TABLE OF CONTENTS

I.   INTRODUCTION

This manual is designed to provide instructors with suggestions regarding course design, lecture planning, model answers, and additional exercises for use with *The Elements of Contract Drafting with Questions and Clauses for Consideration*. The text and this manual provide instructors and students with material for approximately fifty to seventy-five percent of the course time of a two credit hour, fourteen week course or its equivalent. The balance of the time is left for instructors to use in personalizing the course with lecture material, illustrative examples, and problems of their own or those selected from the additional problems contained in this manual. The design is intended to provide adjunct professors and instructors (who are often responsible in large part for teaching courses such as contract drafting) with standardized content and structure while still allowing them freedom to personalize the course and "make it their own." The course materials were developed for either a second- or third-year law school course, but could conceivably be integrated into a first-year law school contracts or legal writing course or a paralegal course covering legal drafting.

Good companion references to this text are *The Redbook: A Manual on Legal Style* by Bryan A. Garner (West 2002) and *A Manual of Style for Contract Drafting* by Kenneth A. Adams (ABA 2004), Thomas R. Haggard & George W. Kuney, *Legal Drafting in a Nutshell* (3rd edition, West 2007). More advanced contract drafting techniques, some at thoughtful variance with the default rules and styles discussed in the text can be found in Howard Darmstadter's *Hereof, Thereof, and Everywhere* of: *A Contrarian Guide to Legal Drafting* (ABA 2002). These books can provide instructors with additional topics for class discussion. Finally, a good assortment of additional problems and exercises relevant to contract drafting can be found in *Legal Drafting: Practical Exercises and Problem Materials* by Thomas R. Haggard (West 1999).

As you teach the course and develop techniques or have comments on this manual or the text - - or any other subject related to contract drafting - - I encourage you to contact me to influence future editions.

Prof. George W. Kuney
The University of Tennessee College of Law
1505 West Cumberland Ave., Suite 202
Knoxville, Tennessee 37996-1810
(865) 974-2500
(865) 974-9921 (fax)
gkuney@utk.edu

1

II. DISCUSSION

A. THE EDIT-LED LEARNING TECHNIQUE: THE DIRECTED EDIT

The text and this manual are based on the belief that one should keep discussion of the contract drafting process short, succinct, and concrete. Lectures are notorious for conveying only ten to thirty percent of their content to students. Also, students are unlikely to do more than skim lengthy reading assignments about writing. Writing is a physical exercise – reading lengthy tracts on the subject is no substitute for engaging in the activity.

As a result, the text consists of brief discussion of the points in each chapter and a few examples of these points. After students have read the materials, a brief lecture recapping the highlights of the section and illustrating them through reference to actual examples (the appendices to the text may prove useful here) should be sufficient to frame the issues and techniques in their minds. At that point, conduct an in-class exercise that covers that same material. This can consist of drafting a short section of a contract, drafting a term sheet, revising or line-editing all or part of a contract, and outlining a contract based upon certain facts and the like, followed by a "directed edit" of the exercise by classmates. The materials have been prepared to support this focused, "read-listen-do" format.

The directed edit consists of having students exchange their work product and then comment and line-edit (in writing) on specific issues announced periodically during the exercise. Divide the issues into five groups: macro, paragraph/section, sentence/word choice, cite form/cross-references/proofing, and substantive issues. This deconstruction of the contract greatly assists the neophyte drafter in organizing the review of the document.

- **Macro issues** include the overall structure and appearance of the document, formatting, use of headings, ordinal ordering systems, overall organization, and tabular form.

- **Paragraph/section issues** include confining each paragraph or section to one subject or task – each paragraph or section should have one and only one "job", proper ordering of sentences within the section (usually from the general to the specific; rules before exceptions), use of sub-paragraphs or sub-sections to further isolate individual mechanisms and provisions, and the like.

- **Sentence/word choice issues** include grammar and similar points, the top three generally being use of the active voice; using "shall clauses" for duties, "may clauses" for rights and options, and "will clauses" for predictive statements; and precise word choice within a plain English structure.

- **Cite form/cross-referencing/proofing issues** are self explanatory; you can not impress upon the students enough the need to carefully proofread to ensure accuracy. Fanatic attention to detail – the hallmark of sophisticated transactional practice – is not a skill that is sufficiently emphasized in pre-legal education.

- **Substance issues** include whether the document is appropriate to the transaction at issue and whether the proper sorts of provisions are used to achieve the desired effects. Perhaps the most important substance issues involve ordering the parties' performances and the interrelationship of representations, warranties, indemnities, covenants, defaults, and remedies. Most students do not encounter these sorts of provisions in their modern form in contracts class. A contract drafting course is a perfect way to move them from an understanding of abstract contract principles to practical, applied contract skills.

In conducting the directed edit, instructors should periodically announce a new issue for the students to seek out and correct or comment upon. For example, one instruction might be "Now look at the overall organization of the document. Is it logical and easy to follow? Do the provisions proceed from the general to the specific?" or "Examine all of the clauses specifying the duties and rights of the parties. Are they correctly presented in the active voice? Are 'shall' and 'may' clauses used appropriately and consistently throughout?" By teaching students to edit and analyze the contract of another, they learn to write their own. As with so many things, it is often easier to see the strengths and weaknesses of others first and then to consider whether one shares those traits rather than merely engaging in isolated self-examination.

These directed edits will (a) help the student editor understand and apply the rules that are being taught; (b) disclose rules that the student editor does not understand, such as the perennial failure to recognize what the

3

passive voice looks like in print, especially in one's own prose; (c) help the student writer get used to having work product reviewed, commented upon and corrected by peers (a.k.a. developing a thick skin for constructive criticism); and (d) assist instructors by providing both an initial pre-grading evaluation of the work and an opportunity to evaluate the work of two students based on a single project.

Do not be discouraged when early in the semester the edits are awful! Concentrate on teaching students the editing skills. As they develop as editors, their own primary work product will improve. This phenomenon is "edit-led learning." In the long run, it cuts down instructors' work as there is less need for direct teaching (read: trying to cram information into students) and more opportunities for learning facilitation (read: responding to specific questions and directing group activity that allows the students to learn for themselves). Edit-led learning seems to work, to one degree or another, with all but the most recalcitrant students.

At the end of the directed edit, which is generally a timed affair, the students return the edited papers to the authors after noting their names as editors on the document. The authors then look over the comments and edits and seek clarification from the editor or instructor on any points that are unclear or in dispute. Then the documents are turned in to the instructor for grading. Both authors and editors are graded on these in-class assignments, providing multiple evaluation points during the course to be used in assigning the final grade. Students' peer pressure, pride, and active involvement in the learning activity appear to increase the amount of material absorbed, reinforced, and retained in and after the course. Similar group edits of completed homework are also effective.

The following is a form that can be distributed to students to guide them through the directed edit process.

Directed Edit Guidelines

Instructions: Identify yourself as the evaluator. Be sure to identify the contract and the drafter. Address, in order:

1. Overall Structure: Is the format good? Is the contract well organized? Do the terms and conditions follow a logical progression?

2. Paragraph/Section/Subsection Structure: Are concepts broken out to make the argument easier to follow?

3. Sentence Structure and Word Choice: Does each sentence make sense? Are the sentences in plain English? Do you think a client would be able to understand the document?

4. Proofreading: Specify each error found.

5. Substantive Effect: Does the agreement accomplish it's goals? Is the client properly represented? Are there any specific clauses that were slanted to the client's benefit? Are there any clauses that improperly benefit the opposing party? Is anything missing?

6. Additional Comments:

B. LONGER ASSIGNMENTS CAN INCLUDE SIMULATED CLIENT INTERVIEWS

Longer drafting assignments can be assigned as homework based upon stated facts. One interesting variation is for the instructor or a student to be assigned the role of a client who has come to the class for a contract. The client expresses her needs for the class in general terms such as "I need a lease so I can sublet half of my office to an accountant," "I need a form lease for audio visual equipment that I want to rent out on a short-term basis to customers," "I want to sell my two-ice-cream truck business that has an exclusive operating permit from the City covering the Excelsior District – What contract should I use?" or "My uncle and I want to form a partnership to buy and operate rental properties – Should we have some kind of agreement?" While these factual situations are perhaps not as realistic as a more complex transaction, perhaps involving millions of dollars and a variety of parties, they are sufficiently familiar or imaginable to students to make the exercise meaningful without lengthy explanations of the substance of a more complex business transaction.

A variation that puts instructors' "war stories" to great use is for the instructor to play the role of a client loosely based upon actual clients or counsel in a past transaction. The class then interviews the client for further details. The facts must be internally consistent, and the students will generally quiz the client on any inconsistency.

It is very helpful if the instructor-client takes off her lawyer hat and expresses herself in lay terms, forcing the students to figure out the appropriate legal classification of the issues and techniques that can be used to address them. Many students find that the hardest part of the exercise is figuring out what they wish to and need to know, how to derive that information, and how to "relate" or create rapport with the client. The instructor can guide the interview at the end to cover any essential areas that have been missed by the students.

After the interview is concluded, the group may then proceed to outline the contract in class and discuss contractual provisions that could be used to address the client's needs. The homework assignment after the discussion is to draft the contract. The students can also be required to keep a record of their time spent in drafting and compute the bill for the services to emphasize the need for efficient work habits if they are to produce legal work product that clients can afford.

6

C. GROUP PROJECTS AND NEGOTIATIONS
ARE FRUITFUL EXERCISES

Unlike the real practice of law and the business world, law school generally suffers from a dearth of group and interactive projects. This is unfortunate because the practice of law is interactive at all levels, involving clients, opposing counsel, opposing clients, and colleagues. No lawyer is an island. Assigning students to teams – e.g., a pair as Buyer's Counsel and a pair as Seller's Counsel – giving them a set of common facts – e.g., the basic information about a business or asset and some authority or range of authority on business issues such as price – and then giving them instructions to negotiate and document the best purchase and sale possible can be very effective at giving them a project that involves group work, negotiation, and drafting skills. An alternative for the brave is to assign one or more students to be the clients themselves and furnish them with the business objectives that they and their lawyers must achieve. As they negotiate and draft the contract or a letter of intent, and then later the definitive agreement, valuable interpersonal skills are developed and related to the otherwise somewhat dry topic of contract drafting. Students seem to respond well to these exercises, however, there is the risk of them spending excessive time on them, so be careful.

The following form can be used to solicit information or individual performances within a team. Letting it be known that you will be asking for their information in advance helps to prevent the "free rider" problem that can develop in group work situations if there is no potential sanction for not carrying one's own weight on the project.

Co-Counsel Evaluation

Name:

Name of Co-Counsel:

1. Please provide comments evaluating the performance of your co-counsel.

2. Please state the percentage of the overall work contributed by your co-counsel. If less than 50% please explain.

3. Please assign your co-counsel a grade for her/his role and participation in the assignment, using a numerical scale of 1-100 and a corresponding letter grade of A+ to F.

4. Additional comments:

The next section provides you with a compressed set of information regarding interpersonal styles and negotiations that you may find helpful in preparing a brief lecture on those points if group exercises like these are to be pursued.

D.   NEGOTIATION AND INTER-PERSONAL STYLES

The following is an outline of lecture notes or talking points for a class on Negotiation and Interpersonal Styles that can effectively set the stage for group work and projects involving negotiations. There are many helpful books available on the subject. Among those books and guides are X.M. Frascongna, Jr. & H. Lee Hetherington, *The Lawyer's Guide to Negotiation, A Strategic Approach to Better Contracts and Settlements*, American Bar Association 2001, ISBN: 1-57073-891-2, and the classic *Getting to Yes: Negotiating Agreements Without Giving In* by Roger Fisher & William Ury, ISBN: 0-14006-534-2. Perhaps the best lesson that can be learned from the latter is the usefulness of pre-negotiation due diligence and preparation about one's own position, resources, needs, and wants.

Lecture Notes on Negotiation and Interpersonal Styles:

Negotiation is a game you can and will play every day--if you do not already.

There are no hard and fast rules – but keep making them up as you go. There are a number of basic, generally-applicable principles that govern in most negotiations.

What you cannot or should not do: break the law, breach applicable codes of ethics, damage your professional reputation, diminish long-term effectiveness by being too successful at this stage of the relationship. Your client may have only a limited understanding of these matters.

Leverage is what drives negotiation. Leverage = Power to change the situation. Leverage changes depending upon the circumstances. What happens if no deal is struck? What happens if the opportunity is lost for the other side? For your side? Will litigation ensue? If so, who will win? Be realistic about both the strong and weak points in all these inquiries.

Manipulate four strategic variables to exercise leverage: uncertainty, time, opportunity, sanction.

<u>Uncertainty</u>. Powerful variable. The fear of the unknown. A negotiated deal or settlement means a decrease in uncertainly; a blown deal represents an increase in uncertainty, perhaps threatening the biggest uncertainty, litigation, which represents the parties' loss of control over their own destinies.

<u>Time</u>. Run the clock. Announce deadlines. Deals happen when they have to happen. If you have more time (or the other side thinks you do) you have more power and more leverage. The party with the most time wins; you get the best deal when you do not have to get one done.

<u>Opportunity</u>. Positive reinforcement – praise behavior that benefits you or your client, but don't waste praise. Do not give up anything without getting something in return. Do not be unreasonably reasonable.

<u>Sanction</u>. "If you do not X then we will Y." Formulate a good sanction. Communicate it effectively and without unduly increasing level of hostility. Then, if no X, you MUST Y.

<u>Personal Style and Interpersonal Relations</u>. People view life as active or passive, and the environment as being either favorable or antagonistic.

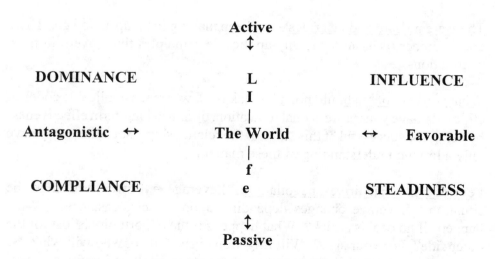

Lots of tests can be done to determine where one falls on this matrix and others like it, but be honest with yourself and determine which of the words marking the end of each axis is more in keeping with your world and personal view. Also remember that, generally, only twenty percent or so of all people view life as "active" – that is twenty percent of "people," not "excellent lawyers" or "successful business people."

Once you know where you stand, figure out where the other side does. There may be more than one answer to this, and it may change over time. The point is not to assume that the other side is a reflection of you. Figure out what "type" is on the other side and appeal to appropriate tendencies or prejudices. Remember, it is a matrix. Folks fall at various points on each spectrum, not necessarily in the middle of a quadrant.

> Dominants. These folks are motivated, self-starting individualists who seek out and enjoy challenges and are generally quite competitive. They think and make decisions quickly and thrive on the unusual. They are unlikely to be able to hold their interest or attention in anything that is routine.

>> Dealing with Dominants: Focus on the point at issue and focus on objective points; demonstrate mutual benefit; emphasize options and results; and document assertions with facts. But do not fail to set deadlines, waste time or deal with needless detail, overstate the case, appear indecisive or unprepared, or assume failure to carefully evaluate is a negative sign.

> Influencers. Think sales people (good ones) – outgoing, engaging, gregarious, persuasive, big on relationships. Often they really want to be liked and trusted and they like and trust those around them (or try to). Performers.

>> Dealing with Influencers: Develop rapport and treat them like equals; be friendly, warm, enthusiastic, and open. Emphasize mutual benefits and opportunities; ask for input, and seek involvement. Pose the situation as one requiring joint problem solving. But do not get right down to business, be abrupt, be put off by interruption, or take lack of concentration as a negative sign.

> Sure and Steadies. Easygoing, relaxed, friendly, but possessive about assets and people in their clan or on their team. When they are being pushed or rushed, they tend to slow things down, sometimes in quiet or unobtrusive ways.

Dealing with Sure and Steadies: Establish rapport; be patient and relaxed; be an active listener (shows interest in process); solicit other side's objectives and concerns; stress reliability; and emphasize and demonstrate sincerity. But don't be erratic, impulsive or impatient, overly aggressive, move too fast, leave out important details, or take hesitancy as a negative sign.

Complyers. Cautious folk that like to proceed in a precise and orderly fashion. They are process-focused, conflict avoiding, perfectionists who want to do everything by the book.

Dealing with Complyers: Appeal to logic; substantiate and document claims and assertions; keep negotiations formal and business-like; address details and fine points; anticipate questions and weaknesses of your position/proposal; and make provisions for problems. But do not be overly familiar or casual, move too fast, make statements without back-up, avoid lots of detail, or take caution or coolness as a negative sign.

Other Aspects of Personality:

Motivation – The key issue to focus on is how to capture it and to generate it in the other side. Money? Fame? Public Acclaim? What is the "driver" of the deal for the other side? Figure it out, and withhold it – or meet it out in little bits – until you get what you want.
Aspiration – Statistically, and within a wide window of reasonableness, those that make higher demands get higher settlements. Open high, end high. But, you cannot manufacture this, and it can be overdone.

The Key to Success Is Preparation.

Do not underestimate the power of the first impression.

You never get a second chance to make a first impression.

Perceptions, not realities, are all that count.

Others will often defer to lawyers to structure discussions.

12

Be skeptical.

Communicate Effectively.

Be precise.

KISS – Keep it simple, stupid.

Say what you need to say, and then stop. Anything extra is free information.

Be an active listener and engage in mirroring behavior (but don't perceptibly fake it!). This is psychologically more appealing to other side. It also increases information retention on your part.

Use interruptions consciously.

Be aware of body language signals such as mirroring behavior, head nods, closed arm positions, and the like.

Do not underestimate the power of silence. Try it. Don't respond and se if the other side will volunteer additional information or concessions. It is remarkably easy tactic that often garners tremendous results.

Intensive Preparation is Key

Find out what your client wants; rank and prioritize. But, stay flexible at all times – do not get locked into a position too early in a negotiation. And until you are at your walk away point (see discussion of the BATNA, below), it is always too early.

There are Deal Points (must haves), Secondary Points (would like to haves), and Trade Points (don't really need & can trade). Identify each group.

Develop a strategic walk away point in advance (and stick to it).

Consult Fisher & Ury, *Getting to Yes* – The concept of the BATNA (Best Alternative to Negotiated Agreement). Rank your alternatives from best to worst, set a minimum, and stick to it. When you get there, walk away.

Information and time are the most valuable assets in negotiation.

Opening Negotiations:

Preliminary discussions: avoiding making the opening offer, the oldest stratagem in the book, is still effective. How to defend against it? Avoid making the first offer or use ranges & variables. Both tactics can be overdone. The opening offer can define the floor or ceiling of the negotiation. Remember, you don't get more than you ask for.

The Opening Move:

Gathers information;

Can build a good relationship;

Defines at least one limit of the deal;

Provides opportunity for the first use of leverage.

Do not fall for the giveaway of "preliminary matters" because you will run out of trade points. Illustration: Opposing counsel contacts you to begin working out the "form" of the documents before the economics and substance have been negotiated by you or the principals. Much of substance is hidden in those "preliminary matters." But, you may want to use this strategy.

Consider how to make the opening and subsequent moves. Direct, in-person contact? If so, where? Telephone? E-mail? Correspondence? Subpoena? draft complaint? lawsuit? Think: control, timing, extent of discussions, ability to terminate the discussion, posturing, the poker face.

Conducting Negotiations

Control of all elements is the key.

Deals get done when they need to get done. The side with more time wins.

Control focus and pace. Make the negotiation wander or remain focused as appropriate. Repetition focuses the other side on your objectives and strong points but can also emphasize weak points.

Listening: It takes effort, but listen to all facets of the communication, form as well as substance. Much information is given away to those that listen and observe carefully.

Never underestimate the power of silence, which can maximize uncertainty on the other side.

Play the game of limited authority ("I will need to check with my boss, my client, etc."). It allows for credible deniability, a hard line approach while sheltering rapport, and a backdoor to gain concessions and then revisit an issue.

Ethics

A review of the ethical rules governing practice in the local jurisdiction is highly recommended because there are considerable variances nationwide. A useful exercise is to compile and distribute these rules, including the American Bar Association's (ABA) model rules and any rules or aspirational standards promulgated by the applicable state, local, or specialized bar, to the students and to then discuss their impact on negotiation strategy and conduct. Ethics and practice vary nationwide to a considerable degree. Tactics that may be acceptable in Orange County, California, may be frowned upon in St. Paul, Minnesota, for example.

"A lawyer shall not materially misstate facts" is the principle. In some formulations, this may or may not include both affirmative statements and omissions. Some things, like statements of value, are traditionally treated as opinions rather than facts. Distinguish between primary facts (like those contained in accurate financial statements) with factual conclusions (like the value of a business); the former is within the prohibition, but the latter may not be.

III. COURSE PLANNING

A. SYLLABI

What follows are exemplary syllabi (1) for a two unit, fourteen week course (2) a ten week summer course and (3) an alternative, concentrated, accelerated course structure incorporating other materials. For a two-class-per week course, divide each class at a logical point. General course ground rules and lecture notes are also included.

Contract Drafting

Required Text: Kuney, *Elements of Contract Drafting with Questions and Clauses for Consideration*. **GET TEXT PRIOR TO THE FIRST CLASS.**

Ground Rules:

1. Attendance is mandatory. Absence will only be excused based on prior written notice approved by the instructor. E-mail counts as written notice. Unexcused absences will detract from your class participation score for grading purposes.

2. Each of your homework and in-class assignments will be graded and will be equally weighted with the assignments in each category. Homework will make up fifty percent of your grade. In-class assignments will make up thirty percent of your grade. Your class participation score will make up the final twenty percent of your grade.

3. It is essential to maintain the highest level of professionalism and polite conduct in class. We will be critiquing each other's work, and appropriate constructive comments should be directed to the work, not at the author.

4. Collaboration on assignments with other students, attorneys, or other persons in or out of this class is prohibited unless specifically assigned by the instructor. On the other hand, you are free to consult any written materials, including form books, exemplar banks, and the like, whether in the law library or elsewhere. Remember to look critically at all examples and forms you use and to tailor them to reflect the standards of this class, including plain English. It is no defense to claim "This is how the form book did it."

	Topic/Assignment	Homework Due & Comments
Class 1	Introduction. Before to Class, Read Chapter 1 of text.	
Class 2	Fundamentals of Contract Drafting and Transaction Planning. Prior to Class, read Chapters 2 and 3 of text.	
Class 3	Document Review and Comments. Prior to Class, read Chapter 4.	
Class 4	Consideration and the Term of the Agreement; Conditions. Prior to Class, read Chapter 5 of text.	
Class 5	Conditions. Prior to class, read Chapter 6 of text.	
Class 6	Representations, Warranties, Covenants, Indemnities, Guaranties. Prior to Class, read Chapter 7 of text.	
Class 7	Events of Default and Remedies. Prior to Class, read Chapter 8 of text.	
Class 8	Boilerplate, Arbitration & ADR, Signature Blocks. Prior to Class, read Chapters 9, 10, and 11 of text.	
Class 9	Letters of Intent. Prior to Class, read Chapter 14 of text.	
Class 10	From Letter of Intent to Definitive Documents.	
Class 11	Amending and Restating Agreements. Prior to Class, read Chapter 13 of text.	
Class 12	Covenants Not to Compete. Prior to Class, read Chapter 12 of text.	
Class 13	TBA	
Class 14	Opinions of Counsel. Prior to Class, read Chapter 15 of text. Wind up.	

Class #1

A. <u>Pre-Class Reading</u>: Materials, Chapter 1 – Fundamental Considerations in Contract Drafting

B. <u>Introductory Remarks</u>:

    1.   Introduce yourself.

    2.   Student Introductions – Go around the class and have the students state their name, year, interests, and why they are taking this course. Some consider this hokey, but it breaks the ice and builds rapport.

    3.   Prepare and hand in sheet of paper with name, year, and preferred e-mail address.

    4.   Go over syllabus, rules, and schedules.

C. <u>Lecture – Chapter 1</u>

    1.   Describe the Deal Time Line.

    2.   Discuss <u>Shelby County v. Van Diest</u> (pp. 7-14), and go over UCC security interest perfection system to clarify context.

    3.   Tabular form and plain English.

    4.   Discuss <u>In re Bassett</u> (pp. 16-20).

    5.   Neatness Counts/Attention to Detail (pp. 21-22). Emphasize these points – many students have not built these skills.

    6.   In-class exercise: Question 1 on p. 22. Go over model answer with overhead or other projector. (Turn in for grade or not, optional with the instructor, but if you are not going to grade it, tell the students this only <u>after</u> the assignment is complete).

N.B.: The fundamental materials in Chapters 1, 2, and 3 are one that are foundational and relevant in future classes. The students do not have enough context in terms of drafting assignments to enable them to internalize and retain these introductory and fundamental concepts at this point. It is best to remind them of the existence of these chapters when assigning future drafting projects. Otherwise, students tend to forget to review these chapters and to apply the principles to their projects.

D. <u>Homework</u>: Assign either Question 2 or 3 on p. 22-23.
      Due at opening of following class.

Class #2

A. <u>Pre-Class Reading Materials</u>:

Materials, Chapters 2 and 3 – The Form of Transactional Documents & Drafting Rules.

B. <u>Homework Due</u>: Students are to hold it for the in class exercise.

C. <u>In-Class Assignment</u>:

> Exchange homework. Student editors conduct directed edit (see p.2 of this manual). Approximately twenty minutes total. Editors and authors names must be on paper. Turn in directly to instructor for review before it is returned next class to the author. (This procedure differs from that used in later editing assignments, where students will return edited work directly to the author for review prior to handing the edited work product into the instructor. It is useful to screen these first edits for appropriateness).

D. <u>Lecture</u>:

    1.   Briefly review topics in Chapters 2 and 3 of the assigned reading and solicit questions. Do not assume that the students have actually read the assigned materials.

    2.   Review a contract to illustrate (may use Appendix 2 of text).

N.B.: The fundamental materials in chapters 1, 2, and 3 are ones to which you should return in future classes. The students do not have enough context in terms of drafting assignments to enable them to internalize and retain these introductory and fundamental concepts. It is best to remind them of the existence of these chapters when assigning future drafting projects. Otherwise, students tend to forget to review these chapters and to apply the principles to their projects.

E. <u>Homework</u>: Question 2 or 3 on p.22-23 (whichever was not assigned in class #1) or similar.

Class #6

A. <u>Pre-Class Reading</u>: Chapter 7 – Representations, Warranties, Covenants, Indemnities, Guaranties.

B. <u>Homework to be turned in</u>: As assigned.

C. <u>In-class Assignment</u>: Swap papers. Directed edit of "final" draft. Return to authors.

D. <u>Lecture</u>: Chapter 7. Carefully cover this chapter. This is generally totally new to the students.

E. <u>In-class Exercise</u>: Do Exercise 1 on p. 87. Discuss.

F. <u>Homework</u>: Redraft directed edit in light of final comments.

Class #7

A. <u>Pre-Class Reading</u>: Chapter 8 - Events of Default and Remedies.

B. <u>Homework Due</u>: Redraft. Hand in.

C. <u>Lecture</u>: Chapter 8. Discuss *Beal Bank*. Show or describe format of notice of default letter (but do <u>not</u> distribute sample).

D. <u>In-class Assignment</u>: Draft a better default and acceleration letter for Beal Bank (Exercise. 1 pp.95-108.).

E. <u>Discuss</u>: Exercise 2 on p. 108.

F. <u>Homework</u>: None.

Class #8

A. Pre-Class Reading: Chapter 9 (Boilerplate), 10 (ADR), and 11 (Signature Blocks).

B. Homework Due: None.

C. Lecture: Go over reading, using exercises.

    1.   Exercise 1 on p. 114 regarding boilerplate. Assign one provision to each student, then let them read through and work out the provision. Go around class and have them report on purpose and import. Discuss variations that might be possible.

    2.   ADR: In-class assignment. Exercise 1, 2 or 3 on p. 124. Swap papers and do directed edit. Turn in.

    3.   Signature blocks. Brief description of text.

D. In-class Assignment:

    Interpersonal Skills & Negotiation. Assign students to Buyer or Seller or Plaintiff and Defendant teams, and distribute simple common fact pattern and confidential client instructions. (Sale of small business, settlement of landlord/tenant dispute or the like – instructor should develop and vary each time class is taught).

E. Homework: Negotiate the terms of the deal and reduce to bullet point list. Bring two copies.

A. Pre-Class Reading: Chapter 14 - Letters of Intent.

B. Homework Due: Bullet point list.

C. Lecture: Letters of Intent (the why and how). Go through Letters of Intent in text and discuss provisions.

D. In-class Assignment: Negotiate bullet point list into Letter of Intent. Can use form from book or start from scratch.

E. Homework: Finalize Letter of Intent.

Class #10

A. <u>Homework Due</u>: Letter of Intent and evaluation of co-counsel and opposing counsel.

B. <u>In-class Assignment</u>: Directed edit of Letter of Intent, return to author, and hand in.

C. <u>Lecture</u>: How to move from a Letter of Intent into definitive documents.

D. <u>Homework</u>: Negotiate and document definitive documents to turn in next class.

Class #11

A. <u>Pre-Class Reading</u>: Chapter 13 - Amending and Restating Agreements.

B. <u>Homework Due</u>: Definitive documentation.

C. <u>In-class Assignment</u>: Directed edit of another team's definitive documents. Return to author and turn in. (This takes about an hour).

D. <u>Lecture</u>: Amending and restating agreements.

E. <u>Homework</u>: Small, but pervasive amendment to deal documents (instructor developed).

Class #12

A. <u>Pre-Class Reading</u>: Chapter 12 - Covenants Not to Compete.

B. <u>Homework Due</u>: None

C. <u>Lecture</u>: Discuss Covenants Not to Compete (briefly).

D. <u>In-class Assignment</u>: Perform one of the Exercises from pp. 132-137. Swap, and perform a directed edit. Hand in.

Class #13

A. <u>Pre-Class Reading</u>: None.

B. <u>Homework Due</u>: None

C. <u>In-class Assignment</u>: Drafting exercise (see sample additional exercises in this manual). Copy, and turn in.

D. <u>Homework</u>: Redraft in class for final homework.

Class #14

A. <u>Pre-Class Reading</u>: Chapter 15 - Opinions of Counsel.

B. <u>Homework Due</u>: Additional exercise as assigned.

C. <u>Lecture</u>: Opinions of counsel.

D. <u>Final In-class Assignment</u>:

Take thirty minutes and provide a ten paragraph list of the ten key principles of contract drafting that we have covered.

Go around the room, and have each student identify and explain one principle he/she used. Then, conduct hard count to see how many others did so. Discuss. Useful to record results on board. This assignment is ungraded. It provides conceptual reinforcement for students and direct feedback for instructor and is a nice way to round out the course.

Intensive Course Syllabus[1]

The class will meet for 10 days on the following schedule:
Tues., May 16
Wed., May 17
Thurs., May 18
Mon., May 22
Tues., May 23
Wed., May 24
Thurs., May 25
Tues., May 30
Wed., May 31
Thurs., June 1

Classes will begin at 9:30 AM and will end at 1:30 PM, except for the last two classes, which will end at 2:30 PM. Classes will be held in room 2M-11.

The first week of the course will focus on contract drafting; the second week will focus on drafting litigation documents.

The description of this course, as stated in the school handbook is:

> This course is designed to expose students to the various types of Legal Writing and Legal Drafting encountered in law practice. Students will negotiate and draft various types of contracts and will receive intensified instruction in the researching and written discussion of complex legal issues. Students will also receive instruction on preparation of litigation papers and written advocacy. There will be approximately eight written assignments, but no term paper or final examination.

---

[1] Thank you to Professor Robin Boyle of St. John's University School of Law. Used by permission.

Textbooks.

To give students a broad experience, we will learn about drafting both corporate and litigation documents. For this reason, I am asking you to purchase two textbooks:

GEORGE W. KUNEY, THE ELEMENTS OF CONTRACT DRAFTING WITH QUESTIONS AND CLAUSES FOR CONSIDERATION Referred to in the syllabus below as "CD."

MARY BERNARD RAY & BARBARA J. COX, BEYOND THE BASICS: A TEXT FOR ADVANCED LEGAL WRITING. Referred to in the syllabus below as "Advanced LW."

Requirements.

This is a three-credit, graded course. Attendance is mandatory. All students are required to log-on to the course webpage and to check the page regularly. On that webpage, I will be posting assignments (in the event you misplace your hardcopies or miss class), PowerPoint presentations previously shown in class (for you to review course content and sharpen your notes), and last minute announcements.

All students are to assess their learning styles. Instructions will be distributed.

Assignments and Grades.

Pass/fail exercises will count towards class participation and these assignments will be given throughout the course. Class participation counts as 20% of the grade. Assignments #1 (contract provision), #2 (contract provision), #4 (complaint), and #5 (interrogatories) each count as 10% of the final grade. Assignments #3 (drafting a contract from head-to-toe) and #6 (drafting an argument) each count as 20% of the grade.

3)   <u>Class Schedule</u>.

Tues. 5/16   **Introduction to Course, Precise and Concise Drafting; Drafting Rules; Form of Transactional Docs**
In preparation for class, read CD, chapters 1 - 3.
<u>Assignment #1</u> assigned – a provision of a lease – CD, page 23 Exercise 3.

Wed. 5/17   **Document Review and Comments; Conditions; Reps, Warranties, etc.**

In preparation for class: Read CD, chapters 4, 6, and 7.
<u>Assignment #1</u> due.
<u>Assignment #2</u> assigned – negotiate and draft provisions of a contract using the concepts of chapter 7.

Thurs. 5/18   **Events of Default and Remedies; Boilerplate**
In preparation for class: Read CD, chapters 8 and 9.
In class: discuss reading and work on <u>Assignment #2</u>.

Mon. 5/22   **Contract Negotiation and Drafting – From Head to Toe**
<u>Assignment #2</u> due.
<u>Assignment #3</u> assigned – negotiate and draft a contract using all of the chapters assigned in CD – a contract from head-to-toe. This assignment may build upon <u>Assignment #2</u>. Begin negotiating <u>Assignment #3</u>.

Tues. 5/23   **Signature Blocks; Covenants and Agreements Not to Compete**
In preparation for class: read CD, chapters 11 & 12.

Wed. 5/24   **Letters of Intent and Opinions of Counsel**
In preparation for class: read CD, chapter 14 and Advanced LW book, chapter 15.

Thurs. 5/25   **Pleadings**

In preparation for class: read Advanced LW book, ch. 11.

Assignment #3 due.

Assignment #4 assigned (complaint).

Tues 5/30   **Notices of Motion, Motions, and Orders**

In preparation for class: Read Advanced LW book, chapter 12.

Assignment #4 due.

Wed. 5/31   **Interrogatories**

In preparation for class: read Advanced LW book, ch. 13.

Assignment #5 assigned (interrogatories).

Thurs. 6/1   **Argument - Last class**

In preparation for class: read Advanced LW book, ch. 10.

Assignment #5 due

Assignment #6 (argument) assigned.

Mon. 6/5   Assignment # 6 due at reception desk.

LEGAL WRITING SEMINAR SYLLABUS

Office room 4-17, tel: (718) 990-6609
Email: boyler@stjohns.edu

Office hours:
TBA

The class will meet Tuesdays and Thursdays from 11:10 AM
– 12:35 PM

The description of this course, as stated in the school handbook is:

> This course is designed to expose students to the various types of Legal Writing and Legal Drafting encountered in law practice. Students will negotiate and draft various types of contracts and will receive intensified instruction in the researching and written discussion of complex legal issues. Students will also receive instruction on preparation of litigation papers and written advocacy. There will be approximately eight written assignments, but no term paper or final examination.

1)   Textbooks.
To give students a broad experience, we will learn about drafting both corporate and litigation documents. For this reason, I am asking you to purchase two textbooks:

GEORGE W. KUNEY, THE ELEMENTS OF CONTRACT DRAFTING WITH QUESTIONS AND CLAUSES FOR CONSIDERATION. Referred to in the syllabus below as "CD."

---

[2] Thank you to Professor Robin Boyle of St. John's University School of Law. Used by permission.

MARY BERNARD RAY & BARBARA J. COX, *BEYOND THE BASICS: A TEXT FOR ADVANCED LEGAL WRITING*. Referred to in the syllabus below as "Advanced LW."

In addition, the following book will assist you in writing concisely:

RICHARD C. WYDICK, *PLAIN ENGLISH FOR LAWYERS*. Referred to in the syllabus below as "PE."

2)   Requirements.
This is a three-credit, graded course. Attendance is mandatory.

All students are required to log-on to the course webpage and to check the page regularly. On that webpage, I will be posting assignments (in the event you misplace your hardcopies or miss class), Powerpoint lectures previously shown in class (for you to review course content and sharpen your notes), and last minute announcements.

All students are to assess their learning styles. Instructions to be distributed.

4)   Assignments.

Pass/fail exercises will count towards class participation. Class Participation counts as 10% of the grade.

All graded assignments will be marked on a scale of 1-10. Each of the Assignments for # 1-7 will count as 10% of the grade. Assignment #8 counts as 20%.

5)   <u>Class Schedule</u>.

Tues., Aug. 23   **Introduction to Course**

Thurs., Aug 25   **Contract Drafting**
- In preparation for class, read CD, chapter 1.
- Discuss <u>Shelby County State Bank v. Van Diest Supply Co.</u> and chapter 1.

Tues., Aug. 30   **Chapter 3 (Drafting Rules)**
- In preparation for class, read CD, chapter 3.
- Discuss drafting rules and do in-class rewriting exercise.
- Bring PE to class – in-class exercises assigned from chapter 2 (Omit Surplus Words).
- Powerpoint presentation on learning styles.

Thurs., Sept 1   **Chapter 2 of CD (Form of Transactional Docs)**
- In preparation for class: read CD, chapter 2; do exercise 2 on page 22 (Nonrecourse Obligation of Loan Agreement) and bring to class. This exercise will be edited by others and handed in.
- In class: discuss assigned reading; and CD, Appendix 3 (Real Property Lease). Begin to work on exercise 3 on page 23 (Assignment or Subletting Provision of Commercial Lease) (<u>Assignment #1</u>).

Tues., Sept. 6   **Chapter 4 of CD (Document Review and Comments)**
- In preparation for class: Finish <u>Assignment #1</u> and bring two copies to class; read CD, chapter 4.
- In class: Students edit <u>Assignment #1</u> and hand-in both copies (<u>Assignment #1</u>); discuss assigned reading.

Thurs., Sept. 8   **Chapter 5 of CD (Consideration) and Chapter 6 of CD (Conditions)**

- In preparation for class: Skim Chapter 5 (much of the subject is covered in other classes and will not be covered in this class); Read Chapter 6 and do exercise 2 on page 73 (Provisions from Contract of Sale).
- In class – hand-in exercise; discuss assigned readings.

Tues., Sept. 13   **Chapter 7 of CD (Reps, Warranties, Covenants, Guaranties, Indemnities)**

- In preparation for class: read CD, Chapter 7.
- In class: Discuss assigned reading; begin in-class exercises – <u>Assignment #2</u> assigned.

Thurs., Sept. 15   Continue with Chapter 7

- In class: complete exercises and <u>Assignment #2</u> due.

Tues., Sept. 20   **Chapter 8 of CD (Events of Default and Remedies)**

- In preparation for class: Read chapter 8.
- In class: discuss reading & begin in-class exercise.

Thurs., Sept. 22   **Chapter 8 – continued**

- In class: continue with in-class exercise and hand-in exercise.

Tues., Sept. 27   **Chapter 9 of CD (Boilerplate)**

- In preparation for class: read chapter 9.
- In class: in-class exercises on chapter 9.

Thurs., Sept. 29   **Chapter 10 of CD (Arbitration, ADR)**

- In preparation for class: read chapter 10.
- In class: in-class exercises on chapter 10.

Tues., Oct. 4   **Chapters 11 of CD (Signature Blocks) and 12 of CD (Covenants and Agreements Not to Compete).**
- In preparation for class: read chapters 11 &12.
- In class: do in-class exercise within chapter 12.

Thurs., Oct. 6   work on contract

Tues., Oct. 11   work on contract

Thurs., Oct 13   **Chapter 14 of CD (Letters of Intent)**
- In preparation for class: read chapter 14.
- In class: do in-class exercise.

Tues., Oct. 18   work on contract

Thurs. Oct 20   **Chapter 15 of Advanced LW book (Opinions of Counsel)**
- In preparation for class: read chapter 15.
- In class: do in-class exercise.

Tues., Oct. 25   **Chapter 11 of Advanced LW book (Pleadings)**
- In preparation for class: read chapter 11
- In class: discuss readings and do in-class exercise. Contract (Assignment 3-4 due). Assignment #5 assigned.

Thurs., Oct 27   **Pleadings continued** – Assignment #5 due.

Tues., Nov 1   No class – All Saints Day

Thurs., Nov. 3   **Chapter 12 of Advanced LW book (Notices of Motion,**

Motions, and Orders)

- In preparation for class: Read Chapter 12 of Advanced LW book.
- In class: discuss readings and do in-class exercise. Assignment #6 assigned.

Tues., Nov. 8   **Chapter 13 of Advanced LW book (Interrogatories).**

- In preparation for class: read chapter 13 of Advanced LW book. Assignment #6 due.
- In class: Discuss readings and in-class exercise. Assignment #7 assigned.

Thurs., Nov. 10   **Chapter 13 continued** – Assignment #7 due.

Tues., Nov. 15   **Chapter 10 of Advanced LW book (Argument)**

- In preparation for class: read Chapter 10 of Advanced LW book.
- In class: Discuss readings and in-class exercises. Assignment #8 assigned.

Thurs., Nov. 17   **Argument continued**

Tues., Nov. 22 Students work independently on Assignment #8

Thurs., Nov. 24   School closed for Thanksgiving

Tues., Nov. 29   **Argument continued**

Thurs., Dec. 1   **Argument** – Last class – Assignment #8 due.

B. CHAPTER-BY-CHAPTER COMMENTARY

The following sections contain brief remarks relevant to each of the chapters and the appendices of this book. They, like the text, are brief and suggestive in nature. Individual instructors should consider doing some background reading on any of the subjects with which they are unfamiliar. They should fill out this material and that in the text with examples from "real life". Examples like this, carefully distinguished from mere "war stories" that lack an illustrative or pedagogical purpose, can make a dry subject like contract drafting come alive.

The text itself is very brief in its discussion of each of these subjects because it is the author's experience that one can not practically expect most students to read long tracts on drafting or writing. This is not to say, however, that the instructor should not do so in order to have the theoretical and practical background to respond to student inquiries. The sources listed in the Bibliography are recommended for this purpose. A prepared and informed instructor that marches the students through the text and its exercises, both homework and in-class, and conducts directed edits with the students can expect them to retain a large percentage of the points made in the text and to emerge from the course with the rudiments, and some nuances, of contract drafting and document review firmly in place.

Chapter 1: Fundamental Considerations in Contract Drafting

This chapter presents the fundamentals of contract drafting. However, a good assumption to make when covering these materials is that the students have never been told any of these things. The lecture and class discussion should feature as many examples as possible. Often the best examples are those with which the students have some passing familiarity: apartment leases, car purchases, and the purchase and sale of residential real estate. The last of these is the classic, understandable example of the deal time line, complete with due diligence.

Shelby County v. Van Diest (pp. 7-14) deals with a classic drafting problem: Different descriptions of collateral in interconnected documents. The case is self-explanatory, but the students may not have a firm grasp of the Uniform Commercial Code (UCC) Article 9 perfection system. It is a good time to go over the process of perfection of a security interest in collateral by filing. Distributing a sample security agreement and UCC-1 filing form is often helpful. Many of the students, even those who aced commercial law, may have never seen these documents.

Discussion regarding the case can take many forms and focus on a number of points. Popular examples include a discussion of ambiguity and whether there is an objective standard for ambiguity; whether two descriptions, one a subset of the other, should simply be interpreted narrowly to mean only the subset or whether there is reason to consider the superset itself; the use and misuse of the cannons of interpretation; the practice of taking blanket liens in all of a debtor's assets instead of limiting a purchase money security interest to the goods purchased and the commercial realities involved in this sort of financing; and whether or not the doctrine of contra proferentem is something that can be relied upon.

Plain English (pp. 15-16) and *American General Finance* (pp. 16 to 20) provide an opportunity to disabuse students of the thought that legal prose should be opaque or confusing. Many students exit their first year of law school with the impression that the use of Latin, confusing and compound sentence structure, and opaque defined terms are the desirable norm for legal drafting. Some students even object to the use of plain English on the ground that they will not sound educated enough. Of course, this is not the case. It is a good time to disabuse them of these notions and to begin emphasizing that contracts, like other legal documents, should be drafted in a plain style that can be understood by lay persons of average intelligence, even if consultation with counsel may be necessary to determine the enforcability of their terms and their interrelationship to other documents and events.

The discussion of attention to detail and pride in one's work (p. 21) bears emphasis because these are habits that have not been widely emphasized in recent years in high school and undergraduate education. Yet, they are at the heart of a lawyer's practice. Emphasizing these habits at this point also provides notice that assignments that are sloppy, filled with typos, or that contain careless errors will be graded down for these attributes.

The discussion of thinking like a transitional lawyer at the end of the chapter provides a good opportunity to introduce students to the other, non-litigation side of law practice. It is a good opportunity to discuss detailed planning for contingencies and making a record between your client and the other side as well as between counsel and the client. Disappointment brings lawsuits and, should that come to pass, counsel should be prepared.

Chapter 2: The Form of Transactional Documents

This chapter is largely self-explanatory and does not contain many Questions and Clauses for Consideration. The exception to this statement is in the section on defined terms, which contains four exercises. These are meant to suggest to students the enormous "macro" power of small, "micro" items like defined terms and to get them into the drafting and planning process. Exercises two and four are based upon *Sigma Fin. Corp. v. Am. Int'l Specialty Lines Ins. Co.*, 200 F.Supp.2d 697 (D. Mich. 2001) (interpreting "Interrelated Wrongful Acts") and *In re Combustion Engineering, Inc.*, 366 F.Supp.2d 224 (D. N.J. 2005). Exercises one and three are drawn from the author's experience and do not appear in a published decision.

Lecturing through the material, identifying the models for future use is often the most efficient mechanism for delivering or reinforcing this information.

Chapter 3: Drafting Rules

Also largely self-explanatory, Chapter 3 states rules that are generally applicable. Covering these rules through lecture and illustrating the points with sample contracts is a useful technique. Perhaps the most important sections of the materials to separate out for in-class discussion are Sections A (the active voice) and D (shall, will, must, and may). These conventions, if adopted early on, will prevent many mishaps in drafting contracts and completing the other exercises in the balance of the materials. Discussion of the Questions and Clause for Consideration (Twenty-Five Contract Drafting Considerations that Comprise a Philosophy) is a good exercise to close the chapter and to move from the micro-focus of this chapter back to the macro-focus of Contract Drafting in general, a nice segue to Chapter 4, Document Review and Comments.

Chapter 4: Document Review and Comments

The material in this chapter is important and difficult to impress upon students. One method is for the instructor to share some examples from their own personal experience to illustrate the points discussed and show how a thick skin and ability to appropriately deal with comments from others (whether those comments are appropriate or not) is an important part of learning how to be a good lawyer, transactional or otherwise. Given the ease of black lining revisions in documents with modern word processors, consider having your students hand in all re-write assignments in back-line (and, if needed, clean) form. It will save you time and teach them a valuable skill.

The section document review (pp. 55-58) can provide guidance that makes for a good group project. If the instructor gives the students a sample contract to review according to the checklist and conducts an in-class discussion of the document's shortcomings and possible remedies for those shortcomings, the students' focus on contract analysis will be sharpened and reinforced. Because there is an abundance of contracts available to any instructor, instructors are well advised to choose one that they already know (so as to know at least some of its nuances). No Questions or Clauses for Consideration are included. If necessary, the first, unrevised version of the Settlement Agreement in Appendix 4 can be used.

Chapter 5: Consideration and the Term of the Agreement

A. Consideration

This is the first of the chapters that examine specific types of provisions common to most contracts. The first section of the chapter, A. Consideration, is self-explanatory and very basic, but do not assume that the students will find it so. Although they have spent time in their contracts class discussing consideration and its adequacy, they have probably spent little time examining or drafting provisions actually providing for it. Similarly, although they may have some notions regarding allocation of consideration, or aggregating it in a multi-part transaction, they probably have little experience drafting such allocation provisions in a clear and concise manner.

B. Allocation of Consideration

Turning to Section B, the notion of allocation of consideration, while perhaps easy to grasp in the abstract, presents some drafting problems for students. Most problems in this area revolve around accurately describing subsets of consideration to provide for all the consideration for and so that each item falls in only one category.

C. Variable Consideration

This is the heart of this chapter and will be the hardest part for the students. It requires them to think through how a transaction is going to unfold and to provide a formula or formulation of the variable consideration that will function properly. Many students will see these problems as being their old nemesis — the word problem from high school and college algebra — coming back to haunt them.

The first problem in the Questions and Clauses for Consideration on page 62, drawn from Howard Darmstadter's article in Business Law Today, is meant to dispel some of these concerns. It is fairly basic, and most of the work has been done for the students. Their main task is fusing the use of equations with the normal contract clause comprised of words. The second and third problems in this set are meant to be a bit more abstract and to force the students to come up with their own (albeit basic) formulas and express them in words or symbols as part of a contract.

The fourth problem in this section is, at least in appearance, one of the hardest in the book. Instructors working with it often say that they could not assign it to the students because they themselves did not understand it. However, although the problem is long and has been rendered overly opaque and apparently complex (one suspects deliberately by counsel to the Maker), once the key to the provision has been found, it, and its trap, are easily understood. Before turning to those features, do note that going over the introduction and background to the problem with the students is fruitful. Most second—year law students have not had the chance to examine and diagram a joint venture real estate development structured as a purchase and sale with a combination of level and contingent payments.

The key to understanding the Participating Contingent Interest provision is, as the text suggests, one of multiple reviews to isolate and understand the important parts of the provision and to sort them out from the detail and chaff. The first section (11.1) is important insofar as it provides the definition of the Participating Contingent Interest and the waterfall[3] of split payments. Mixed in with these portions is an overwhelming amount of detail that is difficult to relate to anything and which, on the first pass, is best ignored. This is especially true of the attractive nuisance that is the Internal Rate of Return "IRR" formula, a prime distractor that can consume much energy and lead to a failure to focus on the truly important features of the provision. Since, in the problem, the students represent the Seller/Lender, they should focus their attention on what it is that triggers the shift in payments from the first tier of the waterfall (100% to Maker) to the second tier (75% to Maker and 25% to Lender) and what it is that triggers the shift

---

[3]The term waterfall is used to suggest that this provision works like a series of cascades flowing from intermediate bowls or pools. Water flows into the first pool (100% to Maker) until that pool is full (target IRR is reached), at which point the water flows in two cataracts, 75%/25%, into two more pools, one for the Maker and one for the Lender/Seller. When the Maker's second pool is full based upon the 75% stream, the pool overflows in two more streams, 50%/50% into two more pools, again one for the Maker and one for the Lender/Seller.

from this second tier to the third tier (50% to Maker and 50% to Lender): *the Maker achieving a particular return (Preferred Return or Additional Preferred Return) on invested capital.*

What determines whether a particular return on investment is achieved? Three possible things:

(1) the revenue generated over a particular time period,

(2) the return desired or required, and

(3) the principal upon which that return is calculated.

The Seller/Lender's counsel should examine each of these areas for the potential for mischief and to ensure that the triggering mechanism for the waterfall provision is understood.

Revenue Generated. There are a number of factors, such as sales volume, timing, quality of product, costs, and the like, that will not be in the Maker's best interests to manipulate such that they harm the Lender. In the end, all these factors affect the financial success or failure of the entire project, an endeavor in which the Maker and Lender's interests are aligned.

The Required Return. The discount rate used for the IRR, although it appears complex and subject to manipulation, especially when viewed by lawyers or lawyers-in-training with math anxiety, is actually the product of a formula that is wholly dependent on revenue generated, the timing of that revenue, and the investment needed to produce it. It is not subject to much controversy.

The Principal Component. By process of elimination, you have probably guessed that this is where the potential for mischief lies. But where? In a real estate development deal, the principal investment like this is generally easy to spot and define. The developer puts down as little cash as possible (the principal investment), receives seller financing for the balance of the purchase price (the level, sum-certain payments referenced in the introductory material), and obtains construction financing for the build-out costs. After all, this is why the Seller/Lender has agreed to subordinate its lien to Permitted Senior Debt. The first sentence of section 11.2 seems to confirm this approach: one notes that Capital Investment means "all capital . . . in excess of [$2 million]." But, it is the second and third sentences that hold the potential for mischief. By including all amounts borrowed by the Maker and all letters of credit obtained that are not secured by the property, if

45

the Maker does not follow the standard (and too easily assumed) model of construction financing secured by a lien on the property being developed, and instead pledges other, non-project collateral, then all sums borrowed, potentially all sums needed to acquire, construct, develop, sell, and market the project will be included in Capital Investment. This could so far inflate the principal invested that the waterfall provision is never activated beyond the first level! In any event, the expected economic return to the Seller/Lender, if evaluated based upon the assumption of the standard construction-financing-secured-by-the-project model, will be dramatically decreased if any non-project-secured financing is used by the Maker/Developer.

The rest of the provision is largely window dressing, providing for details of calculation of the return that triggers the waterfall and the variables involved. If one gets too engrossed in these details before finding the key provisions that can cause mischief for one's client, one may simply get lost in the underbrush. This is an actual provision in use in the commercial world, and its intricacies discussed above have eluded experienced counsel reviewing the provision despite the fact that funding a development with an unsecured loan or a loan secured by property other than the development is not a very sophisticated trick, especially for a large developer with access to institutional credit and public debt and equity markets.

So, what should the students take away from problem 4 on pages 64 to 70?

(1) They need to critically examine provisions from the perspective of their client's interest by, among other things, examining the legal and factual assumptions that underlie their conclusions.

(2) They have the ability to work through even the most seemingly difficult provision and find its key features through a process of successive, more focused reviews. The Document Review checklist on pages 56-58 can provide a mechanism to guide their review.

(3) They should develop the confidence not to be scared by voluminous legal prose or word problems, yet retain the caution and prudence to understand that things are not always what they seem and that downside risk to their client must always be thoroughly evaluated.

D. *The Term of the Agreement*

After the prior section, this section represents a conceptually easy wind-down to Chapter 5. Contracts are effective over some period, and the beginning and end of that period must be ascertainable. Further, just because the contract is not yet or is no longer effective in some sense does not mean that some duties are not in force; termination does not mean that everything is done. These are the basic points to be made here. The exercises are simple for experienced lawyers, but force the students to think through these fundamentals.

Chapter 6: Conditions

The chapter on conditions provides an opportunity to heighten micro-drafting skills. The text encourages students to closely tie conditions to consequences of satisfaction or failure to do so and to use plain English in the process. The effect and effectiveness of "best efforts" and "time is of the essence" clauses are discussed. Both exercises focus on these points. The first is shorter and deceptively easy, but forces the students to confront problems with defined terms that can arise when multiple parties may elect to occupy the position of the announcing or offering party.

A case that can supplement the text for those seeking additional material is *Wurtsbaugh v. Banc of America Securities LLC*, 05 Civ. 6220 (DLC) (S.D.N.Y. June 20, 2006). There, Banc of America Securities LLC was held not to have breached a merger contract when it bought a securities order-execution firm and then "frustrated" its growth by selling off its own companion trade-clearing business before making all the contingent payments to the sellers, ruled the U.S. District Court for the Southern District of New York. Judge Denise Cote, pointed out that the sellers "failed to contend with" the best efforts clause's own limiting language, which says that nothing in the merger agreement shall "limit in any manner whatsoever" BOA's conduct of its business or its control of the target company. First, the court dismissed the sellers' claims that BOA breached the best efforts clause and its duty of good faith and fair dealing. It rejected their contention that BOA breached the clause by not "promoting and assisting" their efforts to increase DAF's business, by reassigning DAF's sales force, improperly reclassifying new DAF clients as preexisting BOA clients, and by firing Wurtsbaugh without cause when the merger contract states that he can only be fired for cause. The sellers, the court noted, failed to contend with the clause's limitation language. "Reading the Best Efforts Clause to require [BOA] to utilize the DAF Division in particular ways or to refrain from terminating Wurtsbaugh, an at-will employee [under his separate employment agreement]," the court said, "would impose limitations on both the conduct of [BOA's] business and its control of the DAF Division." Additionally, the court rejected the sellers' claim that BOA breached its duty of good faith and fair dealing. "In order to find that [BOA] has breached its duty," the court said, "it would be necessary to read into the Agreement an obligation that [BOA] make business choices with the growth of the DAF Division in mind. Implying such an obligation under the Agreement would be inconsistent with the limiting language of the Best Efforts Clause and is thus beyond the scope of the duty of good faith and fair dealing." This "unambiguous language," she said, "requires dismissal of the claim based on an alleged breach of the Best Efforts Clause."

Chapter 7: Representations, Warranties, Covenants, Guaranties, Indemnities

This and the next chapter are the most doctrinal of those in this text. Students will have been made loosely familiar with some of these terms in their historical or common law sense, but most have not been exposed to all of them nor have they been exposed to their modern forms and uses. One of my colleagues refers to representations, warranties, covenants, and indemnities as the "Four Horsemen of the Contract" — a pun on the classical painting "The Four Horsemen of the Apocalypse" featuring anthropomorphic representations of Conquest, War, Famine, and Death. She is right. Like the classical four horsemen, these provisions, if deployed properly, tie together and have a cohesive overall effect ensuring both performance and the meeting of expectations or, failing that, the right to recover damages for the shortfall. As such, students should focus on the unique aspects of each sort of provision and how they can or cannot tie together. The exercises are geared to this end.

Focusing the students on the evolution of a proposed unqualified representation and warranty to one featuring knowledge, qualifications, materiality thresholds and other limitations is critical. Here, as well as in chapter 6, best efforts clauses are discussed.

Chapter 8: Events of Default and Remedies

This chapter is largely self-explanatory. It bears pointing out, however, that although most second-year students are well acquainted with the concept of breach of contract and suits to compel performance or obtain a judgment for damages based upon a breach, they are not well acquainted with the substitute for breach and all the common law rules relating to such suits: the default and remedies section of a modern contract. Explore the use of default/remedies provisions, how they substitute for concepts of breach, and how a suit to enforce the contract and its default and remedies is often the modern alternative to a suit for breach. The *Beal Bank* case provides an opportunity to explore some of these notions, underscores the need for clear drafting of things like notices of default and acceleration, shows the dangers of precatory[4] language, and provides an opportunity for the students to devise a notice of default and acceleration that would have prevented the dispute at issue.

Chapter 9: The Import and Scope of Boilerplate

This is a short, straightforward chapter. Most of the discussion is best focused by examining a sample boilerplate and redrafting it, as appropriate. Reference to the appendices can be useful for additional examples.

Chapter 10: Arbitration and Other Alternative Dispute Resolution Provisions

It seems like every law school text on Contracts must discuss alternative dispute resolution "ADR" processes. This one is no different, except that a perhaps more jaundiced view is taken of binding arbitration in this text when compared with some others. The text is fairly explicit on these points. Whatever the instructor's feelings about arbitration, the point to emphasize with these materials is that the level and type of ADR should be the product of thoughtful choice and careful drafting, not knee-jerk incorporation of provisions from prior documents.

The final two exercises in the chapter provide an opportunity to explore both ethical issues and standards of practice.

Chapter 11: Signature Blocks

This chapter is self explanatory.

Chapter 12: Amending and Restating Agreements

There are two ways to use this chapter in class. The first is short and sweet: describe the three methods of amendment discussed in the text and when they are useful. The second is a bit more doctrinal and is suitable for

---

[4] "Precatory . . . adj. (of words) requesting, recommending, or expressing a desire for action, but usu[ally] in a nonbinding way." Black's Law Dictionary 1195 (7th ed. 1999).

those instructors with an interest in constitutional law and a class with enough background in that subject to participate in the discussion. Those instructors may find it useful to review the redlined version of the constitutions and discuss the changes that the Confederate government made to the original, ranging from spelling, capitalization, and punctuation to substance, the disputes and case law that gave rise to these Confederate "draft arounds." In the right setting, an animated discussion of amending the social contract to deal with such topics as abortion, gun control, state support of religion, equal rights for women and other minorities, federalization of criminal and commercial law, and the like can emerge.

Chapter 13: Covenants Not to Compete

Covenants Not to Compete get their own chapter in the text because most law students are exposed to these provisions as first-years. Thus, they generally have more of a general understanding of the transaction and the applicable substantive law than is the case with other types of contracts. As a result, covenants not to compete provide a good stopping point for drafting and reinforcing the skills from prior chapters in what should be a comfortable factual and legal setting.

Chapter 14: Letters of Intent

The focus of this chapter is on letters of intent and other interim agreements that contemplate more formal, final documentation at a later date, which may or may not ever be drafted. Here, we refocus on the deal time line and the context in which lawyers draft. When covering this material, instructors may want the students to negotiate and draft a letter of intent based upon specified facts and, then, convert it into definitive documents.

The *Beekman* case presents a good summary of the state of the law regarding letters of intent and agreements to agree. Internal citations have largely been edited out for brevity.

Chapter 15: Opinions of Counsel

This is a "for-your-information" chapter and in no way delves into the intricacies of third party opinion practice. It is important, however, for all students of transactional drafting to understand the role of opinions of counsel, as they are becoming part of all but the most routine transactions. The *Dean Foods* case covers the basics and can serve as a warning to new attorneys about the dangers of playing fast and loose with legal opinions, at least if the court sees it that way. This is a good chapter to cover in a last class before the wind-up and recap of the course that most instructors like to deliver.

The following chart was prepared by and is used courtesy of Susan Irion, formerly of Northwestern University. It makes a nice overhead to sum up after chapters 6 & 7.

Representations, Warranties, Covenants, Conditions, General Propositions

	Representations	Warranties	Covenants	Conditions
What	Statement of presently existing facts	Promise that facts are as stated	Promise to act/not act in future	Something that must be satisfied before another legal obligation exists
When Effective	Date contract executed; may terminate at closing	Closing	At time covenant to be performed	Only triggers duties or rights
Purpose	Induces entry to agreement	Establishes facts	Creates duties, including duty to fulfill warranty	Prevents legal consequence to a party if other party doesn't meet condition
Typical Remedies	▪ Damages as of signing (pre-closing) ▪ Maybe tort remedy if fraud or misrepresentation (could include punitives) ▪ Rescission pre-closing ▪ Restitution (of deposit, etc.)	▪ Damages as of closing or sale ▪ Maybe tort remedy if fraud or misrepresentation ▪ Rescission post-closing	Damages (usually compensatory), or specific performance, as of time covenant to be performed	None (must be coupled with duty) (Except that a constructive condition is a promise and condition)
Limitations	May be qualified, e.g.: 1) materiality (often $ amount), or 2) knowledge of particular person as of date certain	Same as representations	May be qualified as to: 1) Best efforts 2) Commercially reasonable efforts 3) Etc.	May, as stated, apply to: • conduct of parties, or • external events
Drafting Basics	Use present tense Combine representations and warranties	Same as representations	Use "shall" for duties and "may" for rights Use active voice Cover who, what, when, where, why, how	Conditions as to conduct: use "must" or "if" Conditions as to event: use "if," "when," or "after" Sellers may want objective conditions; Buyers may want subjective

*Not intended to be complete statement of law in any jurisdiction

Compiled by Susan Irion, based upon the text:
George W. Kuney, *The Elements of Contract Drafting:
With Questions and Clauses for Consideration* (West Group 2003)

IV.   SAMPLE ANSWERS

The following answers are based upon actual student responses to the exercises in the text. They are "sample" in the sense that they represent answers that can be examined and critiqued. They are not offered as the best answers to the problems, all of which can have multiple and varied answers. Some even contain problems and ambiguities that seem to arise with each class that tackles the exercise.

When conducting in-class exercises or after collecting homework, it is useful to project a model answer to the exercise (one from these materials or one of your own) using an overhead projector or document camera so that it can be discussed by the whole class while the exercise is fresh in their minds. For this reason, each of these model answers is on a separate page.

In recent years, with the proliferation of laptops and wireless internet access it has become possible to have the students compose answers in class and e-mail them to the instructor for projection and in class commentary and editing on the fly.

Page 21–Exercise 1:

> A series of losses arising from the same event shall be treated as a single loss in the application of the deductibles. However, notwithstanding the foregoing, in the event of losses to property arising out of which separate deductibles are applicable, then such deductibles will be applicable by class of property as if the losses had occurred separately.

MEANING: One event with many losses = single loss for deductible
(purposes).

But, if those many losses are spread across different classes of property set out elsewhere in the insurance policy (e.g., vehicles, inventory, equipment, which each have separate deductibles), then apply each deductible to each class.

WHOM DOES THIS CLAUSE BENEFIT?

Both Parties. First sentence, the insured; Second, the insurer.

MODEL LINE-EDIT REDRAFT:

Back-line: (I) A series of losses arising from the same event shall be treated as a single loss in the application of the deductibles. However, ~~notwithstanding the forgoing~~, in the event of losses to <u>multiple classes of</u> property ~~arising out of which~~ <u>each having</u> separate deductibles ~~are applicable~~, then such the deductibles will be <u>applied class by class.</u> ~~applicable by class of property as if the losses had occurred separately~~.

Which results in:

Clean: (I) A series of losses arising from the same event shall be treated as a single loss in the application of the deductibles. However, in the event of losses to multiple classes of property each having separate deductibles, then the deductibles will be applied class by class.

CONCEPTUAL REDRAFT:

Think: When there are many losses from the same event, apply the deductibles once, class by class. Hey, this is not about a series of losses (as the original wording of the provision might suggest)! It is about application of deductibles! Try to write it to focus on its real purpose.

Write: Each deductible shall be applied only once (to each class of property) to a loss or losses caused by the same covered event.

          The conceptual re-write substantially reduces the length and complexity of the provision and increases reader comprehension.

Page 21–Exercise 2:

The provision is a non-recourse provision from a real estate financing transaction. It means that the principals, officers, and employees of the borrower are not personally liable on the loan (i.e., there is no "recourse" to them) and that, in the event of default on the loan, the lender is restricted to recovering by foreclosure on the collateral.

Original Provision:

Section 2.10. *Nonrecourse Obligation.* Without releasing, impairing, forgiving or waiving in any manner or amount the obligations or promises of the Borrower or any other party contained, referred to or defined in the Loan Agreement or the Financing Documents, and without releasing, impairing, forgiving or waiving the right to foreclosure of the Mortgage for the full amount of all indebtedness evidenced by the Loan Agreement and by the Mortgage, which right of foreclosure, by any lawful means, as to real and personal property described or referred to therein, is specifically reserved by the Loan Agreement, the covenants and agreements of Borrower to make the payments required under the Loan Agreement and under the Financing Documents shall be without recourse to any partner of Borrower, or any officer, director, employee or agent of any partner of Borrower. Upon the occurrence of an Event of Default, neither the Trustee, the Issuer nor the Bondholders shall take any action against the partners of the Borrower except such action as may be necessary to exercise any and all rights and interests the Trustee or the Issuer may have in and to any and all collateral securing such indebtedness and to subject such collateral to the satisfaction of such indebtedness. The provisions of this Section 2.10 shall not apply to the Borrower's indemnification obligations under Section 4.1 hereof.

Model Answer #1:

Section 2.10. *Nonrecourse Obligation.*

2.10(a).	No Partner in the Borrower or any person or entity named in the Loan Documents is [or shall be] personally liable for the obligations and liabilities of the Borrower under the Loan Agreement and Financing Documents. This section does not affect the obligations of any party contained in the Loan Agreement or Financing Documents or the right of any party

	to foreclose the Mortgage for the full amount of the debt as provided in the Loan Agreement and the Mortgage.
2.10(b).	In the event of a default under the Loan Agreement or Financing Documents, the Trustee, Issuer, and Bondholders shall not take any action[, legal or otherwise,] against the Partners or other persons or entities named in the Loan Documents except as may be necessary to exercise any rights against or to the collateral securing the Debt.
2.10(c)).	The provisions of Subsections 2.10(a) and (b) do not apply to the Borrower's indemnification obligations under Section 4.1 of this document.

Model Answer #2:

[From a student who embraced the tabular form. This model answer can be used to discuss taking a good thing too far and whether that has happened here.]

Section 2.10. *Nonrecourse Obligation.*

    (a)   Borrower or any other party in the Loan Agreement or the Financing Documents shall not release, impair, forgive, or waive:

        a.   any obligations or promises in the Loan Agreement or the Financing Documents; or

        b.   the right to foreclosure of the Mortgage for the full amount of all indebtedness arising from the loan Agreement and the Mortgage.

    (b)   Borrower's covenants and agreements to make payments under the Loan Agreement and Financing Documents shall be without recourse to any:

a. officer, director, employee, or agent of the Borrower;

b. partner of the borrower; or

c. any partner's officers, directors, employees, or agents.

(c) The Trustee, Issuer, and Bondholders shall not take any action against the partners of the Borrower except as may be necessary to foreclose upon and realize value from the Collateral.

Page 21–Exercise 3:

Article XI
Assignment or Subletting

Model Answer:

I.   Restrictions on Assignment or Subletting by Lessee

        A.   Without first attaining the written approval of the Lessor, the Lessee shall not:

               (1) Assign, or permit assignment of, this Lease, whether by mortgage, operation of law, or otherwise;

               (2) Sublet any portion of the leased premises; or

               (3) Permit a third party to occupy the whole or any part of the leased premises.

        B.   The Lessee shall attain prior written consent from the Lessor for each individual proposed assignment or sublease described above.

        C.   The Lessor shall not unreasonably withhold or delay written consent for Lessee's request to assign or sublet the leased premises. However, the Lessor's consent is subject to the approval of any Mortgagee of the premises, or the Land or Building including the premises, and the Lessor's consent will therefore not be given to the Lessee until the Mortgagee first provides its approval to the Lessor.

        D.   If the Lessee obtains consent to assign or sublease the leased premises, the Lessee is deemed to guarantee the prompt and timely payment of all rent, additional rent, and other charges required under this Lease.

II.   Lessor's and Mortgagee's Consent

        A.   The Lessor or the Mortgagee may not reasonably withhold consent for any proposed assignment or sublease to:

(1) An affiliate of the Lessee; or

(2) Any other reasonably creditworthy proposed assignee or subtenant.

B.   The Lessee must acquire consent from the Mortgagee for any proposed assignment or sublease to a non-affiliate of the Lessee. If the Lessor provides such consent, the Lessee and Guarantor shall have no further liability under this lease.

C.   No act of consent (including acceptance of rent), by the Lessor, to a proposed assignment or sublease by the Lessee, shall constitute consent to any future assignment or sublease by the Lessee, the Assignee, or the Sublessee. Also, no other indulgence or favor granted by the Lessor to the Lessee shall constitute consent to future assignment or sublease.

III.   Additional Payment Required Upon Assignment or Sublease

A.   The Lessor shall only provide written consent for an assignment or sublease if the Lessee agrees to pay to the Lessor one half of the excess (if any) of the annual base rent payable under such sublease or assignment over the Annual Base Rent, on a per-square-foot basis, as designated in this Lease.

B.   The Lessee shall make this payment to the Lessor on a monthly basis, as rent is paid to the Lessee under the terms of the sublease or assignment.

C.   Before making payments to the Lessor, the Lessee may deduct the cost of any initial improvements from the excess rent if such improvements are required in order assign or sublease the premises.

D.   The Lessee shall not be required to make monthly excess rent payments to the Lessor if:

1.   The Lessee sells its entire business (whether by sale of stock or assets), or sells substantially all of the tangible assets of either the industrial or clock business; and

2.   The result of this sale is that the entire leased premises, or a portion of the entire leased premises that is attributable to the industrial or clock business, is subleased to the purchaser.

IV.   Restrictions on Actions of Assignee or Sublessee

A.   No assignment or sublease by the Lessee is valid unless the Sublessee or Assignee agrees, in writing and directly with the Lessor, to be bound by all of the obligations of this Lease.

B.   Therefore, the Sublessee or Assignee shall agree, without limitation, to the obligation to pay rent and other amounts due under this Lease.

C.   The Sublessee or Assignee must also agree in writing to the prohibition, as described in this Article, upon further assignment or subletting of the leased premises without the written consent of the Lessor.

D.   The Lessee, Sublessee, and Assignee shall be deemed to waive any suretyship defenses.

Page 30-Exercise 1:

SNACK CAKE

In order to define a snack cake it is necessary to think about exactly what a snack cake is. A snack cake can be defined by the nutritional content or lack thereof. A snack cake can be defined by the shape and size of the actual 'snack cake' such as in reference to a Twinkie by saying cylindrically shaped and measuring 4" x 1". A snack cake can be defined by the ingredients that are used in each individual snack cake and the baking and/or cooking methods used to make such snack cakes. A snack cake can also be defined by simply breaking down the two words, "snack" and "cake" into their respective definitions.

There is no real easy answer when attempting to define a snack cake because the word "snack cake" encompasses many different products of different shapes and sizes and of varying degrees of nutritional value. Snack cakes are also made with many different ingredients from chocolate to creme to cheese to marshmallows to oatmeal. Anther problem that exists when trying to define a snack cake is the simple fact that there are so many of them with very clever names and only a slight variation in the actual product. In order to get an encompassing legal definition of a snack cake that prohibits them from school vending machines it is necessary to combine the varying aspects of a snack cake into a blended definition.

DEFINED TERM

1.   "Snack Cake" or "snack cake" means, foods that are primarily classified as junk foods that have little or no nutritional value and are not seen as contributing towards general health and nutrition. A snack cake consists of prepackaged snack food that is high in calories but low in nutritional value. A snack cake will be considered as such if the total calories per serving exceed 200 or more than 30% of the total calories are from fat or more than 30% of the total calories are from sugar or more than 8% of the total calories are from saturated fat or if it contains any trans fat or if it contains more than 225 mg of sodium or if it has more than 20 mg of cholesterol.

_____

This definition is primarily focused on the nutritional value that each individual snack cake possesses. The definition listed above does not prohibit snack cakes in an individual vending machine but merely sets the maximum limits on various (select) contents that many, if not all, snack cakes will possess in order for them to be edible and therefore marketable. The definition is more technical in some respects and requires a nutritional background in order to figure out if an individual snack cake falls within or outside the parameters listed above. It can get rather complicated because the packaging and serving size of the many individual snack cakes that are available on the market can vary greatly.

If this law became widespread I can assume that many manufactures would simply develop smaller snack cakes in order for them to individually fall within the nutritional requirements listed above. Instead of getting two cupcakes from an individual package the manufacturer would simply make smaller cupcakes and repackage them so the consumer would get three or four smaller cupcakes that individually would meet the criteria listed in the definition above. This definition is a good starting point because it does set some basic health and nutritional guidelines that define a snack cake. Nutritional values alone will not suffice because of the wide variations in snack cake contents and packaging. It is important to remember the ultimate goal in passing such a law by the legislature.

The ultimate goal as I see it is to increase the health of the youth in this nation and to help them develop good eating habits. With that thought in mind it is necessary to develop a definition for a snack cake that does more than merely require a snack cake to be simply "less unhealthy." The goal as I see it is to limit the school vending machines to only "healthy" foods and snacks as the term "healthy" is commonly understood. It is important to incorporate the appropriate content and language that is fully encompassing in order to keep snack cakes or what one might call "junk" food out of school vending machines.

---

2.   "Snack Cake" or "snack cake" means any product listed as snack cake, or any product with a label or marketing materials that contains the following terms or words or phrases, in any order or phonetic spelling: pies, doughnuts, toaster, pastries, rice, corn, corn cakes, cakes, pretzels, cookies, swiss, rolls, coffee, bones, funny, ring, dings, doodles, brownies, chocolate, cupcakes, cremes, shortcake, nut, loaves, donut, fudge, rounds, gingerbread, maple, marshmallow, shortbread, pecan, oatmeal, crunch, cosmic, peanut butter, cheese, crackers, cherry, treats, delights, pumpkin, frosted, caramel, fig, bars, yodels, twinkies, hohos, dingdongs, Suzy Qs,

donettes, muffins, honey, banana, pound, golden, blueberry, iced, pecan, maple, shortbread, puffs, fillings, cinnamon, crumb, pipettes, powdered, rich, butter, puffs, twist, lemon, twist, heaven, danish, raspberry, walnut, sundae, fudge, coffee, super, vanilla, coconut, chip, loaf, bars, pound, blueberry, muffins, holes, napoleon, dog, or balls.

I have looked at and analyzed the top seven snack cake brands which are Little Debbie, Hostess, Private Label, Tastykake, Drake's, Dolly Madison, and Entenmann's. A common thread runs through the naming of these products. Most of the products have similar names or at least contain many of same words in some order. The list that I put together is very inclusive. I did not want to say in my definition that it is inclusive but it is difficult to find a product name that does not contain one of the words listed above in some fashion. This form of a definition has a few advantages over the previous one. For instance, the drafter can list many more terms than I did in order to make it almost exhaustive. The drafter is able to not only limit how "unhealthy" an item will be but the drafter can simply and easily include those items which are "unhealthy" and that are considered junk food and not appropriate for the school vending machines.

Another benefit of this form of a definition is the fact that it is simple in many respects. The reader can look to see if a product contains the words listed in the definition and if it does then the product is excluded from the vending machine. It does not take a dietician to figure out if a product contains a word that is on the list. I tend to like lists in a definition especially for a definition that is complicated because it gives the reader some idea about what the drafter is contemplating. In this instance, the drafter can meet with those that represent the interests of the students or school board and go over the products that they want to exclude from the list and simply list them for all to read.

The problem that I see in formulating this definition is that some products contain subtle variations of words or phrases that mean nothing in terms of what the product contains. For instance, I came across a type of pie from a smaller company that was called Moon Heaven. It contains chocolate, marshmallow, and creme. I did add 'heaven' to the list but it is words or phrases like this that are used to describe products that might slip past the drafter. It can also become prevalent for the manufactures to start naming their products differently. This is unlikely to come from the big manufactures because they have such name recognition already established with their brands and it would be foolish to retool their whole marketing campaign in an effort to establish a new brand identity. This problem might be more prevalent from smaller local manufactures of snack cakes and could present a way around the draft as it stands written.

---

3.   "Snack Cake" or "snack cake" consists of prepackaged snack food that is high in calories but low in nutritional value. Prepackaged snack cakes as defined below shall be considered as such regardless of the use of "light" or "low fat." A "Snack Cake" or "snack cake" shall mean any prepackaged singular item regardless of how packaged and marked which is made with dough, flour, sugar, eggs or baking powder, baking soda, or beaten eggs, shortening, or any leavening agent. "Snack Cake" or "snack cake" will be considered as such if the total calories per serving exceed 200 or if an individual unit per package as sold exceeds 100 calories regardless of serving size as indicated on the package. A "Snack Cake" or "snack cake" will be considered as such if more than 20% of the total calories are from fat or more than 20% of the total calories are from sugar or more than 5% of the total calories are from saturated fat or if it contains any trans fat or if it contains more than 200mg of sodium or if it has more than 10mg of cholesterol as indicated on the package or as applied to an individual unit per package as sold. A "Snack Cake" or "snack cake" will be considered as such if it does not contain nourishing ingredients, such as whole grains or is not fortified with nutrients such as calcium or potassium. "Snack Cake" or "snack cake" means any product listed as snack cake, or any product that contains the following term(s) or word(s) or phrases in any manner, respect or position, in the singular or plural, in any order or phonetic spelling thereof including ingredient listed or ingredients used in the manufacturing of the product. Such term(s) or word(s) or phrases include but are not limited to the following: pies, doughnuts, toaster, pastries, rice, corn, corn cakes, cakes, pretzels, cookies, swiss, rolls, coffee, bones, funny, ring, dings, doodles, brownies, chocolate, cupcakes, cremes, shortcake, nut, loaves, donut, fudge, rounds, gingerbread, maple, marshmallow, shortbread, pecan, oatmeal, crunch, cosmic, peanut butter, cheese, crackers, cherry, treats, delights, pumpkin, frosted, caramel, fig, bars, yodels, twinkies, hohos, dingdongs, Suzy Qs, donettes, muffins, honey, banana, pound, golden, blueberry, iced, pecan, maple, shortbread, puffs, fillings, cinnamon, crumb, pipettes, powdered, rich, butter, puffs, twist, lemon, twist, heaven, danish, raspberry, walnut, sundae, fudge, coffee, super, vanilla, coconut, chip, loaf, bars, pound, blueberry, muffins, holes, napoleon, dog, or balls.

This definition is a blend of definition one and two. It incorporates the use of both nourishing information and the use of words to limit the products that can be sold in a vending machine. It also makes references to general concerns of health that should be considered when deciding what products are acceptable to be placed in the school vending machines. General concerns for the health of children or the nutritional value of the foods that they obtain from vending machines can be interpreted very broadly and allows the proponents of this legislation to have much flexibility in how they decide what is "nutritional." In addition, this definition incorporates the use of language that speaks to how certain foods are made and the ingredients that are used to produce such food. The list of ingredients that I used are found in many of the 'snacks' that are to be considered snack cakes for this exercise.

This definition appears on its face to be very limiting and there might be concern that it is too limiting. I am not a dietician, although I have spoken to one for this assignment, but it is possible with a strict reading of this definition to have a severely limited vending machine in terms of the 'snack' options that are presented to school children. The goal of this legislation was to ban snack cakes from the school vending machines not to ban the vending machines altogether. If the goal was to ban vending machines from the school district that could have been simply stated in a singular sentence. This definition can constructively ban vending machines and that is not the goal of the school district.

Like any law that is written it is necessary to find a balance. A theoretical balance does not always apply to the 'real' world and the practical impact of this definition might be too far reaching. Trying to determine what products meet the criteria of the definition listed above is beyond the scope of this assignment but I am sure there are good, fine, healthy foods that can be incorporated into the vending machine for consumption during school hours. If the big snack cake manufactures ever see a decline in sales because they find themselves banned from school vending machines I am sure they will make the necessary adjustments to their products. The big manufactures will then race to exploit the new market and in doing so will improve the health of the youth in this country and that is what this law and definition is aiming to accomplish.

[could use of a tabulated list have made these definitions more user friendly? Do any of these approaches work for this definition? Discuss.]

Page 30-Exercise 2:

"Interrelated Wrongful Acts"

From Sigma Fin. Corp. v. Am. Int'l Specialty Lines Ins. Co., 200 F.Supp.2d 697 (D. Mich. 2001), some discussion:

1. Definition of "Interrelated Wrongful Acts"

The 1998-99 policy states that it provides $1 million in coverage for "Each Wrongful Act or series of continuous, repeated or interrelated Wrongful Acts." Policy No. 244-27-00, Pl. Exh. A.5 Additionally, the policy defines "Wrongful Act" as "any negligent act, error or omission." *Id.* at 2.

AIG argues that this language is not ambiguous, and that there was a single/interrelated/continuous wrongful act - Sigma's sale of MCA products. In contrast, Plaintiff argues that each sale of MCA product was a separate and distinct act. The parties do not dispute the fact that Sigma sold a variety of MCA investment products, including debentures, mortgage pools, and real estate pass-through certificates.

The Michigan Supreme Court has not interpreted the terms "continuous", "repeated" or "interrelated acts", as is used in insurance policies. Additionally, the Sixth Circuit Court of Appeals has not ruled on the issue as presented by Michigan courts. Accordingly, the Court must "attempt to ascertain how that court would rule if it were faced with the issue." *Meridian Mutual Ins. Co. v. Kellman,* 197 F.3d 1178, 1181 (6th Cir. 1999), *rehear'g and suggestion for rehear'g en banc denied,* Feb. 4, 2000. In doing so, "the Court may use the decisional law of the state's lower courts, other federal courts construing state law, restatements of law, law review commentaries, and other jurisdictions on the 'majority' rule. . . ." *Id.* There is no consensus on the correct way in which to interpret this language.

The Court will now discuss and distinguish two decisions from U.S. Courts of Appeals in other circuits.

In *Gregory v. Home Ins. Co.,* 876 F.2d 602 (7th Cir. 1989), the policy at issue provided that, "*two or more claims arising out of a single act, error,*

---

[5] This language is also contained in the 1999-2000 policy. *See* Policy No. 278-15-39, Pl. Exh. B.

omission or personal injury or a series of related acts, errors, omissions or personal injuries shall be treated as a single claim." Id. at 604 (emphasis in original). The U.S. Court of Appeals for the Seventh Circuit noted that the underlying class action arose out of a 1980 offering for sale by Producer's Brokerage Company (PBC) (the client of Home Insurance's insured) of episodes in a videotape series. . . PBC acted as broker of the videotapes. The videotapes were sold individually to investors, most of whom, at the time of sale, also signed a promissory note and a production service agreement authorizing PBC to market the purchased videotape on behalf of the buyer.

Id. at 602-603. PBC hired Steven Gilbert to handle the sale of the videotapes. Mr. Gilbert also drafted an opinion letter for PBC advising that the videotapes were not securities and therefore did not require registration with the Securities and Exchange Commission, and that purchase of the videotapes would receive tax deduction benefits. The Internal Revenue Service disagreed with Mr. Gilbert, and "disallowed the income tax deductions claimed by the buyers of the videotapes, and assessed interest and penalties against them." Id. at 603. Thereafter, plaintiff purchasers of the videotape filed a class action against PBC, which cross-claimed against Gilbert's law firm. Defendant Home Insurance Company, the law firms' professional liability carrier, assumed defense of the case.

The Seventh Circuit was required to decide if Home's insurance policy was ambiguous, and if the claims at issue were related under the insurance contract. The Indiana law regarding ambiguity in insurance contracts provided: ambiguity in an insurance contract exists when [the contract] is susceptible to more than one interpretation and reasonably intelligent [persons] would honestly differ as to its meaning. An ambiguity does not exist simply because a controversy exists between the parties, each favoring an interpretation contrary to the other's. If the court does not find ambiguity in the language of the contract, it will be given its ordinary and plain meaning.

Id. at 604 (quoting *Anderson v. State Farm Mut. Auto Ins. Co.,* 471 N.E.2d 1170, 1172 (Ind.App. 3 Dist.1984)). The Seventh Circuit did not find the policy language as to "related acts," set forth, *supra,* at page 8, to be ambiguous.

As to whether claims against a policy are "related" (*Gregory* policy), or "interrelated" (instant policy), it is noteworthy that all of the sales in

Gregory involved one specific item -- the videotape and an accompanying opinion letter of attorney Steven Gilbert. Given these facts, the Seventh Circuit found the claims brought against the insured to be related. The Seventh Circuit noted: "the individual buyers' claims all arose from the same conduct of Mr. Gilbert," and held that "the word 'related' covers a very broad range of connections, both causal and logical." 876 F.2d at 605-606. The Seventh Circuit concluded that "the rule requiring insurance policies to be construed against the party who chose the language" does not require "such a drastic restriction of the natural scope of the definition of the word 'related.' Parties are generally free to include language of their choice in contracts, and courts should refrain from rewriting them." 876 F.2d at 606.

However, in the instant case, Defendant chose to use the term "interrelated" in the policy's coverage cover-sheet. Thereafter, the policy does not include a definition of interrelated in its "Definitions" section. The instant motion deals with the limits of coverage, so the language of the coverage limits is controlling. The Court concludes that the Defendant's choice of the term "interrelated wrongful acts" in the instant policy, contrasted to use of "related acts" in the *Gregory* policy, is more restrictive as to what is excluded from the benefits of aggregate coverage. In Webster's II New Riverside University Dictionary 1988, "related" is defined as "connected" (p.992), while "interrelated" is defined as having a "mutual relationship" (p.638). Given these definitions, the Court concludes that while many situations may be "related" -- connected in some manner -- significantly fewer situations will be "interrelated" -- involving a mutual relationship. Thus, while all Sigma sales of MCA product might have some connection under the broader term "related," they do not have mutuality or interrelatedness, because each sale included differing types of MCA product sold by different brokers to different customers. Accordingly, the Court holds that Sigma's sales of MCA product were not "interrelated", the term of coverage utilized in the policy drafted by Defendant.

Defendant's policies use the term "interrelated" on the coverage face sheet, but thereafter use the term "related" in Exclusion "j." Exclusion j deals with the policy year which a claim will be assigned, excluding from coverage any claim arising from the "same or related Wrongful Acts," for which a claim had been previously reported under a prior policy, or for which notice had been given under a previous policy year. Defendant interposed Exclusion j in its argument relating to whether the 1998 policy governs all MCA related claims against Plaintiff. Exclusion "j" is discussed *infra* at Pp. 15-16. excluding from coverage any claim arising from the same or related Wrongful Acts, which had been reported or for which notice had been given under a prior policy term.

The U.S. Court of Appeals for the Eleventh Circuit followed the reasoning of *Gregory* in *Continental Casualty Co. v. Wendt,* 205 F.3d 1258 (11th Cir.), *rehear'g denied,* April 19, 2000, a *per curiam* affirmance of a district court opinion, appended to the appeals court decision. The facts, as contained in the district court opinion, were that Bernard Wendt sold promissory notes to investors for a company called K.D. Trinh, and also provided legal services regarding various aspects of the transactions. Wendt and Thomas P. Hall, the lawyer who encouraged him to sell K.D. Trinh promissory notes, were sued in two separate lawsuits. In the second lawsuit, Wendt filed a third party complaint against Hall. Hall's insurance provider brought a declaratory action requesting that the court determine whether or not it was obligated to provide coverage for the third party complaint. The policy language at issue provided:

Any claim or claims arising out of the same or related wrongful acts, shall be considered first made during the policy term in which the earliest claim arising out of such wrongful acts was made.

Id. at 1260 (appendix). In reaching its decision, the court noted that there is disagreement among courts as to the ambiguity of the word "relate." The court found *Gregory* to be persuasive, and concluded:
The words "relate" or "related" are commonly understood terms in everyday usage. They are defined in the dictionary as meaning a "logical or causal connection between" two events. *See* Webster's Third New International Dictionary (1981). There is no ambiguity unless one is *created* through the device of simply ignoring one half of the definition.

Id. at 1262 (appendix) (emphasis in original). The court ultimately concluded that the first lawsuit and the third party complaint were related for the purposes of the insurance policies. The court was not confronted with facts indicating the sale of differing types of K.D. Trinh investment product, nor was it confronted with the policy's use of the term "interrelated".

Plaintiff relies upon the unpublished decision of *Stauth v. National Union Fire Ins. Co. of Pittsburgh,* 1999 U.S. App. LEXIS 14006, 1999 WL 420401 (10th Cir. June 24, 1999), to support its claim that the language at issue is ambiguous. In *Stauth,* the policy used the term "interrelated," the term used in the instant policy. The *Stauth* insurance policy defined the term "interrelated wrongful acts." The policy stated that: "All such causally connected errors, statements, acts, omissions, neglects or breaches of duty or other such matters committed or attempted by, allegedly committed or attempted by or claimed against one or more of the Insured Persons shall be deemed interrelated Wrongful Acts." *Id.* at **4. The instant policy has no such definition. The court in *Stauth* noted that there are "two general lines of authority dealing with the term "interrelated acts" in insurance policies." *Id.* at **7. The *Stauth* court noted that the case before it did not clearly fall into either line of interpretation.

According to the court in *Stauth,* the first line of interpretation involves policies which do not further define the term [interrelated acts], leaving it to the courts to ascertain the meaning. . . . Most courts faced with such policy language have generally taken a pro-insured approach to defining "interrelated," and have held that "legally distinct claims that allege different wrongs to different people" are not "interrelated" claims.

Id. at **7, 1999 U.S. App. LEXIS 14006 at *21. (quoting *National Union Fire Inc. Co. v. Ambassador Group, Inc.,* 691 F. Supp. 618, 623 (E.D. N.Y. 1988)). Additionally, many of the courts that take this approach do so because of the legal maxim that ambiguous terms in an insurance policy should be interpreted in favor of the insured. *Id.* at **8, 1999 U.S. App. LEXIS 14006 at *22.

The second line of interpretation involves policies which further define the term "interrelated." *Id.* For example, some policies state that "interrelated wrongful acts" means Wrongful Acts which are the same related, or continuous; or Wrongful Acts which arise from the same, related, or common nexus of facts. Claims can allege Interrelated wrongful acts regardless of whether such Claims involve the same or different claimants, Insureds, or legal causes of action.

Id. (quoting *Specimen Policy Forms For Lawyers Professional Liability Coverage in New York, Practicing Law Institute: Litigation and Administrative Course Handbook Series* 580, at 516 (1998)). According to the court in *Stauth,* "courts interpreting these specific definitions have been much more willing to find acts to be 'interrelated.' Some of these courts have even concluded that 'but for' causation is enough, under such policy language to render two acts 'interrelated.'" *Id.* at **9.

The *Stauth* court then stated that the policy before it did not fit into either of the two lines of reasoning, because it defined the term "interrelated wrongful acts," using the unspecific term "causally connected." After attempting to define the term "causally connected," the court held that it was a "judgment call" whether to use a narrow or broad definition of the term. *Id.* at **10, 1999 U.S. App. LEXIS 14006 at *29. As a result, the court held that it would construe the policy against the drafter, and hold that the actions were not causally connected. *Id.*

Plaintiff also relies on *David v. American Home Assurance Co.*6 an unpublished case from the Southern District of New York. In *David,* the court stated that the terms "same," "essentially the same," and "related," are not "unambiguous." *David,* 1997 U.S. Dist. LEXIS 4177, 1997 WL 160367 at ** 3. However, because New York law allows for the court to look to extrinsic evidence to determine the meaning of ambiguous terms, and because no discovery had taken place, the court did not construe the term against the insurance company. Rather, it decided to deny the motion to dismiss to allow time for discovery.

As to the instant case, applying the facts of the claims -- different purchasers of different types of security product at different times -- to the undefined term "interrelated" in Defendant's policies, the Court finds that the language of the policies at issue as to "interrelated wrongful acts" is ambiguous. Indeed, while the term "related" may, as set forth in *Wendt,* be commonly understood, Defendant's choice of a different term, "interrelated," undefined in the instant policy, is not such a commonly understood term.

To restate the issue before the Court: are the claims at issue in the instant case part of a "series of continuous, repeated or interrelated Wrongful Acts." Policy No. 244-27-09, Pl. Exh.

The Court finds that the lawsuits brought against Sigma by its customers, based on the failure of MCA, as to which Sigma initiated notice to Defendant, do not constitute the same wrongful act, nor are they part of a series of continuous, repeated, or interrelated wrongful acts.7 Each sale of

---

6 1997 U.S. Dist. LEXIS 4177, 1997 WL 160367 (S.D. N.Y. April 3, 1997).

7 *See, e.g., Federal Deposit Insurance Corp. v. Mmahat,* 907 F.2d 546 (5th Cir. 1990). In *Mmahat,* an attorney was sued for malpractice for advising a client to make loans in violation of the Federal Home Loan Bank Board

MCA product involved different Sigma representatives, different MCA products, and different purchasers. This is not comparable to Sigma selling uniform shares of X Company stock. The Court concludes that the sales of MCA product cannot be considered "continuous, repeated or interrelated Wrongful Acts."

---

regulations. 907 F.2d at 549. These regulations restricted the amount that a savings and loan (S&L) could loan any one borrower. *Id.* The attorney instructed the client to "never [to] turn a loan down because it is over our loans to one customer limit[]." *Id.* The attorney gave this advise so that his law firm generate fees on the closings. *Id.* The law firm was ultimately found liable for $ 35 million in bad loans. *Id.* The insurance policy at issue had a $ 1 million limit for single claims and a $ 2 million limit for aggregate claims. 907 F.2d at 553. The insurer argued that the single limit ought to apply because the attorney carried out a "series of related acts." *Id.* The court rejected this argument. The Court noted that "a single motive does not make a single act," rejecting the argument that the acts were logically connected by the attorney's single motive to generate fees for the firm. 907 F.2d at 554. The court found three discrete acts of malpractice regarding the legal advice which "resulted in discrete losses on seven loans." *Id.* As such, the aggregate limit applied. *Id.*

Page 30-Exercise 3:

"Appeal"

From a stipulated forbearance agreement: ...The Judgment Claim shall become an Allowed Claim upon entry of a Final Order of the Bankruptcy Court setting forth its allowed amount after completion of any and all appeals of the Judgment and the expiration of any period within which to file any further appeals of the Judgment. The Bankruptcy Court shall, upon motion enter an order setting forth the allowed amount of the Judgment Claim. The allowed amount of the Judgment Claim shall be the principal amount of the Judgment, in the amount affirmed after all appeal rights have been exhausted, plus interest at the rate provided under applicable non-bankruptcy law.

Are petitions for review in a state Supreme Court or petitions for a writ of certiorari covered? Check your law dictionary or applicable procedural rules. The answer may well be "no".

Page 31-Exercise 4:

Unless Big Financial holds a power of attorney from these individual or they sign on to the agreement the answer is probably "no". So, it is a broad release on one side and a narrow release on the other. Do you think this is the "intent of the parties?" Why or why not? See In re Combustion Engineering, Inc., 366 F.Supp.2d 224 (D. N.J. 2005).

Simple Formulas in Contracts. This exercise is based upon concepts and discussions from Howard Darmstadter's article "The Arithmetic Lawyer" in Business Law Today (ABA November/December 2000).

A clause from a debt security reads, in part:

Issuer shall make monthly payments to holders of bonds equal to the product of (I) the product of (x) the bond rate and (y) a fraction the numerator of which is the actual number of days in the related interest period and the denominator of which is 360 and (ii) the certificate principal balance as of the close of business on the last day of the preceding interest period.

Cumbersome but understandable if you take the time to decode it:

$$\text{Monthly Payment} = \text{Bond Rate} \times \frac{\text{\# of Days in Period}}{360} \times \text{Principal Balance}$$

Since you need to resort to this or similar mathematical notation to understand the clause, why bother to encode it in words in the first place? It is an invitation to mistakes in the encoding or decoding process. In these circumstances it is better to draft the clause using defined terms and formulas. Try it. Draft provisions requiring an issuer to make the required monthly payments and providing for calculation of those payments using mathematical notations as appropriate.

Model Answer:

7.1   Issuer's Monthly Payments

(a)   Issuer shall make monthly payments to bondholders according to the following formula:

$$\text{Monthly Payment} = \text{Bond Rate} \times \frac{\text{\# of Days}}{360} \times \text{Principal Balance}$$

(b)   Where:

(i)   "Bond Rate" means that rate of interest as stated on the face of the bond;

(ii)   "# of Days" means the number of days in the

preceding calendar month; and

(iii) "Principal Balance" means the Certificate Principal Balance (as defined in section ___) on the last day of the preceding calendar month.

CONSIDERATION

- In order to be enforceable, a contract must be supported by mutual consideration. Consideration in business transactions can take many forms including:
  - Cash
  - Promissory notes
  - Letters of credit
  - Transfers of property
  - Services
  - Transfers or surrender of rights
  - Assumption of another's duty or liability
  - Mutual promises

COPYRIGHT ASSIGNMENT AND ROYALTY AGREEMENT

This COPYRIGHT ASSIGNMENT AND ROYALTY AGREEMENT (the "Agreement") is entered into and effective as of [date], at [city], [state], by and between _____ (the "Author"), and _____ (the "Publisher"), on the basis of the following facts and constitutes a contract of a copyright assignment and royalty payment between the parties. The Author and Publisher are collectively referred to in this document as the "Parties."

RECITALS

A.   The Author has determined that it is in her best interest to enter into this Agreement, whereby the Author will assign to the Publisher a copyright, for a royalty fee and on the terms and conditions set forth below.

B.   [Recitals as appropriate]

AGREEMENT

The Parties agree that the above Recitals are true and correct to the best of their knowledge and the Parties do now further AGREE as follows:

SECTION 1

COMPENSATION

1.   As compensation for Publisher's services hereunder and for the rights granted herein, Author assigns to Publisher her copyright in _____ in exchange for a ("Royalty") of 20% of the ("Gross Revenues").

2.   Publisher agrees to pay Author, semi-annually on September 15 and May 15 each year, a sum equal to twenty percent (20%) of Publisher's Gross Revenues from Publishers publication, distribution and sale of the work _____ .

Gross Revenue. The term Gross Revenue shall include all forms of income derived from Author's copyright assignment in _____ , including all sales revenue directly or indirectly attributable to the publication of _____ including professional or complimentary printed copies of _____ which are distributed gratuitously for advertising, promotional or exploitation purposes. Gross Revenue shall include all printed, published, and sold works in the United States Canada, and Europe by the Publisher or its affiliates, for which money has been received by the Publisher, or been finally credited to Publisher's account. Gross Revenue shall include the above less all returns, credits, and refunds.

Royalty. Payments made to the Author for the right to publish and distribute her copyrighted work. Publisher shall compute the royalties earned by the Author pursuant to this agreement within sixty (60) days following the end of each semiannual calendar period during which monies are received or finally credited with respect to the Author's work, and shall thereupon submit to the Author the royalty statement for each such period together with payment for the royalties due. The payments to the Author provided for under this agreement shall be computed as of September 1 and May 1 for each year in question and shall be paid in United States currency by the Publisher to the Author on or before September 15 and May 15 each year.

PERCENTAGE RENT PROVISION

- Provisions for variable consideration are appropriate when the consideration will depend upon future events.
- Such provisions can include formulas such as percentage of rent provisions.
- Provisions can include adjustments to base consideration depending upon the amount of assets such as receivables or inventory on hand when the sale transaction closes.
  - It might be necessary to include an example to illustrate the workings of a complex formula or adjustment provision.
  - The Real Property Lease below that deals with percentage of rent does not entail a complex formula and providing an example might do more to confuse then to help understand.

REAL PROPERTY LEASE

THIS LEASE ("Lease"), made at _____, _____, on the _____ day of _____, 20____, between _____(the "Landlord"), and _____, (the "Tenant"). Landlord and Tenant are collectively referred to in this document as the "Parties." This lease creates joint and several liability in the case of multiple Tenants. The Parties agree as follows:

1. Premises. Landlord hereby leases the Premises to Tenant, and Tenant
hereby takes from Landlord, those certain premises locates in _____, and outlined on the Exhibit attached hereto ("Premises"), which are located at _____.

2. Term. The term of this Lease (the "Term") shall commence on the _____ day of _____, 20____(the "Commencement Date"), and end on the _____ day of _____, 20 ____ (the "Ending Date"), inclusive.

3. Monthly Rent. Tenant agrees to Pay Landlord as rent for

the Premises the annual amount of $ _____ ("Rent") each month in advance on the first day of each calendar month thereafter during the Term at: _____, or at any other address designated by Landlord. Rent shall be payable in United States legal currency and shall be payable by either: (i) United States Mail or (ii) in person at the address designated by Landlord. If the term of this lease does not start on the first day of the month or end on the last day of the month, the rent will be prorated accordingly.

4.   Percentage Rent. In addition to the Monthly Rent due to
        Landlord on the
1st day of each calendar month Tenant shall pay to Landlord an additional Percentage Rent of 5% of its Quarterly Gross Sales ("Sales") over $500,000 payable quarterly, 60 days after the close of each calendar quarter. Tenant shall provide to Landlord a financial statement showing Quarterly Gross Sales for the prior calendar quarter along with the Percentage of Rent then due and payable to Landlord within 60 days after the close of each calendar quarter. The Landlord shall have the exclusive right to audit the Tenant from time to time at Landlord's own expense in order to verify the accuracy of each financial statement. If any such audit of Tenant's financials reveals that Tenant has understated Sales by more than 2.5% than Tenant shall incur the cost and pay for such audit and pay to Landlord an additional fee of 1% of actual Sales for the period in which the audit was conducted.

5.   Sales. The calculation of Quarterly Gross Sales for the purposes of Percentage Rent shall not include Internet sales. Additional deductions from gross sales prior to calculating Percentage Rent shall include sales and excise taxes, returned merchandise, credit card fees, employee sales, and sales of things other than normal merchandise.

Page 64 – Exercise 4 – The Waterfall:

A. The Developer is proposing a situation where it will have the right to any profits made from the development. Based on the criteria of 1.1(a), the Developer will recoup its Capital Investment plus a 15% return on any Capital Investment it puts into the development. Section 11.1(a) states that "Distribution of Cash Flow . . . shall be deemed to be made first with respect to accrued and unpaid Preferred Return, with the balance applied and credited to Developer's Capital Investment." Additionally, 11.1 further states that if the Developer later makes an Additional Capital Investment, then Preferred Return, Preference Capital, and Additional Preferred Return, and thus distributions of Excess Cash Flow, are calculated from the additional investment. Under these scenarios, any additional capital investments and/or distributions of cash flow are credited to the Developer's Capital Investment and the Developer is then earning interest on interest. Money is continually being added to the Developer's Capital Investment and the required return must be met before the Seller has the opportunity to receive the participating contingent interest. Basically, the provisions are set up to look as if the Seller will be able to share in the profits of the development. The reality of the situation, however, is that the Developer will receive the Excess Cash Flow distributions.

B. The Seller (original landowner) bears the risk because he does not have any possibility of receiving the "equity kicker" if the project doesn't go well.

C. The Seller's participating contingent interest is essentially eliminated if the Developer uses its own funds to finance the development rather than borrowing funds from a third party (as the seller probably assumes will happen). The more principal the Developer puts in, the more money the Developer gets out. The definition of Capital Investment explains this because it includes money the Developer supplies, as well as any amount the Developer borrows and spends on the property, and any letters of credit it obtains in connection with acquiring and developing the property. Thus, the Developer's incentives are to use as much principal as possible to develop the property. If the Developer does this, the payments of the participating contingency interest are never triggered. Basically, the distribution of cash flow won't get past 1.1(a) and the Seller never receives any distributions.

D. Redraft: 11.1 <u>Payments of Participating Contingent Interest</u>. As additional consideration for the sale of the Property by Seller to Developer, Seller shall be entitled to receive certain additional payments based on the cash flow generated from management, sales, and operations of the Property. The payments received by Seller under this Section 11 are called "Participating Contingent Interest." In order to calculate payments of Participating Contingent Interest to Seller, a third party will hold and periodically distribute Cash Flow and Excess Cash Flow (as defined below) to Seller and Developer according to the priorities outlined below. Excess Cash Flow (defined as Cash Flow remaining after payment of any required payments of Unpaid Purchase Price under this Note or any optional payments made under section 6) shall be distributed periodically as follows:

(a) First, payments of Excess Cash Flow shall be made to Developer until Developer has received "Preference Capital" distributions based on the following formula:

Preference Capital = Distribution = Developer's Capital Investment + Preferred Return

Preferred Return = 15%(Developer's Capital Investment)

Distribution of Cash Flow under this section shall be deemed to be made first with respect to accrued and unpaid Preferred Return, with the balance applied and credited to Developer's Capital Investment.

(b) Second, Excess Cash Flow shall be distributed as follows:

(1) 75% to Developer
(2) 25% to Seller

Until time when Developer has received "Additional Preferred Return" based on the following formula:

Additional Preferred Return = Distribution = Until both X and Y are achieved.

83

X = (Preference Capital + (Developer's total Capital Investment – Developer's Excess Capital Investment))25%; and

Y = 200%(Developer's total Capital Investment – Developer's Excess Capital Investment)

(c) Thereafter, Excess Cash Flow shall be distributed equally between Developer and Seller.

Distributions of Participating Contingent Interest are made pursuant to subsections (b) and (c) above. If Developer later makes an additional Capital Investment ("Additional Capital Investment"), then Preferred Return, Preference Capital, and Additional Preferred Return are calculated from and after the date that the Additional Capital Investment is made. Also, distributions of Excess Cash Flow shall be made based on the priorities outlined in Section 11.1 with respect to Preferred Return, Preference Capital, and Additional Preferred Return payable with respect to such an Additional Capital Investment. The Seller shall not be required to return any payments of Participating Contingent Interest paid to Seller on account of such an Additional Capital Investment under any circumstances.

For purposes of this Promissory Note, the term "Internal Rate of Return" or "IRR" means the annual discount rate, determined by iterative process, which results in a net present value of approximately zero (0) when the discount rate is applied periodically to Developer's Capital Investment and certain distributions in respect to Developer's Capital Investments. For purposes of determining IRR for this agreement, the formula below shall be utilized:

$$NPV = -CC + \frac{1}{1+r} + \frac{1}{(1+r)^2} + \ldots + \frac{1}{(1+r)^n}$$

"-C" = Developer's Initial Capital Investment.

"C_n" = Developer's additional Capital Investment invested in the period denoted in subscript.

NPV = Zero.

r = Periodic discount rate expressed as a decimal is equivalent to the annual "IRR" or internal rate of return.

For the purposes of the above formula, Developer's Capital Investment made in any month shall be treated as having been made on the first day of the month and cash distributions in any month shall be treated as having been made on the last day of the month.

In the event of a sale of all the Property by Developer in agreement with the terms of this Note and the Deed of Trust, to the extent all of the consideration shall not have been paid in cash, the collection and distribution of Excess Cash Flow, as to when and to the extent received, shall be administered and distributed by the Developer according to the provisions of section 11.1 above. In the event Developer has been dissolved, the former managing member of Developer shall assume responsibility for administration and distribution of Excess Cash Flow according to the provisions of section 11.1 above.

Participating Contingent Interest, if any, shall be payable monthly on or before the fifteenth business day of each calendar month.

11.2 <u>Definitions</u>.

    (a)   <u>Capital Investment; Definition</u>. The term "Capital Investment" shall mean any and all capital, including Excess Capital Investment, contributed by the members of the Developer in excess of $2,000,000, as and to the extent spent by the Developer on and after the Closing Date as defined in the Purchase Agreement with respect to the acquisition, construction, development, and sales and marketing of the Property. Capital Investment shall also include any amounts borrowed by Developer and not secured by the Property, as and to the extent the loan proceeds are used for the acquisition, construction, development, and sales and marketing of the Property. Capital Investment shall also include letters of credit obtained by or on behalf of Developer and delivered in connection with Developer's acquisition and development of the Property ("Letters of Credit"). However, the collateral is limited to the Property and none of Developer's members have any liability for such letters of credit. Thus, unless amounts are drawn by the beneficiary of a Letter of Credit, the outstanding liability amount of such Letter of Credit shall not be deemed Capital Investment for purposes of calculating Preferred Return and Additional Preferred Return, and shall not be included in the principal amount of any Capital Investment.

(b)   Cash Flow; Definition. "Cash Flow" for any calendar month is defined as Revenues during the month plus any cash reserves maintained by Developer that Developer reasonably, and in good faith business judgment, determines to be unnecessary and therefore releasable, less the sum of:

    (i)   Costs during the calendar month;

    (ii)   Deposits into reserves (if any) made during the month; and

    (iii)   Payments required and made during the month under the Permitted Senior Debt Documents.

(c)   Costs; Definition. "Costs" shall mean, for a given calendar month, the aggregate of the following which are properly chargeable to the operation of the Property and as determined under the cash method of accounting unless otherwise provided in the document.

    (i)   Real estate taxes and insurance premiums paid;

    (ii)   Service payments; maintenance contract payments; development fees; on-site employees' wages and fringe benefits; costs of repairs and maintenance; promotional and advertising payments; public relations and similar expenses; reasonable accountants' fees; fees and expenses of third party operators of the "Facilities" as defined below; and other reasonable operating expenses of the Property accrued during such calendar month;

    (iii)   With respect to sales of the Property and Memberships, all reasonable and customary costs and expenses incurred by Developer in connection with the sales of the Property and Memberships, including reasonable attorneys' fees of Developer, Seller, and Senior Lender, title insurance, reasonable travel and entertainment expenses, and brokerage fees at prevailing market rates;

(iv) Justified and reasonable refunds paid by Developer during the calendar month of any Revenues received in an arm's length transaction.

(v) Reasonable administrative and general overhead expenses of Developer and its managing member for expenditures incurred directly in connection with the operation and development of the Property.

(vi) The actual costs of restoration of the Property incurred following a casualty to the extent of the permitted deductible under the applicable insurance policy or where there are no insurance proceeds and Developer is not required to and does not carry insurance.

(vii) Costs of construction and other hard costs to the extent not paid with advances under the Permitted Senior Debt; and

(viii) Actual fees and other costs of issuance paid to the Permitted Senior Debt.

"Costs" shall not include fees, expenses, interest, Preferred Return, or other consideration paid by Developer (or any of its Affiliates) with respect to debt or equity capital contributed by members of Developer. "Costs" shall include market rate fees paid to the issuers in respect to the issuance and/or renewal of Letters of Credit.

(d) Excess Capital Investment; Definition. The term "Excess Capital Investment" shall mean any amount by which Developer's Capital Investment exceeds $_____.

(e) Revenues; Definition. "Revenues" shall mean, for a given month, all Revenues from the Property and its operation, as determined under the cash method of accounting, received by Developer or its authorized managing agent for the Property during that calendar month. "Revenues" shall, without limitation, include the following:

(i) All consideration (including, when converted into cash, promissory notes or any other form of consideration) actually received by Developer from all sales of the Property. Consideration shall also include any forfeited deposits retained by Developer (in the case of terminated escrow), option fees to purchase lots or monetary settlements with prospective purchasers;

(ii) Fees and revenues generated to Developer from the operation of those certain country club and golf course facilities ("Facilities") to be developed on the Property, including receipts with respect to charges for merchandise, services, rents, license fees and from all other sources derived by Developer (or its Affiliates) from the Facilities;

(iii) Fees for lessons, greens fees, tennis court fees, public and private banquets held at Facilities, membership dues and all other fees or charges of any kind paid with respect to the use of the Facilities;

(iv) Brokerage commissions, fees and any proceeds retained by Developer (or its Affiliates, but excluding the Sales Company referenced at Section 16.1 of the Purchase Agreement) in the transfer or sale of memberships or interests in the Facilities;

(v) Charges for all food served and sold at the Facilities, including alcoholic and non-alcoholic beverages;

(vi) Fees and revenues generated to Developer (or its Affiliates) in respect of the sale of membership interests in the Facilities and the sale of the Facilities, as may be permitted under the Deed of Trust;

(vii) Proceeds from financing, refinancing and further encumbrancing the Property as and to the extent permitted under the Deed of Trust, including, without limitation, the Permitted Senior Debt proceeds; and

(viii) Any other funds or proceeds received from any other source derived from the Property, including casualty insurance proceeds and condemnation proceeds not applied to restoration of the Property.

Page 70–Exercise 1:

    1.   Draft a provision establishing an effective date for a contract that is the date it is signed by all parties. Assume that the document has been drafted according to the basic structure given in these materials, and that the term "Contract" was defined in the first paragraph.

Model Answer #1:

A.   <u>Effective Date</u>. This Contract shall be effective and binding on the parties on the first date that it is signed by all of the parties.

Model Answer #2:

B.   <u>Effective Date</u>: This Contract shall be effective as of the date it has been signed by all of the parties.

2. Draft a provision providing for termination of a contract one year from its effective date unless it is renewed by the parties at least a month before it would otherwise expire.

Model Answer:

20. <u>Termination</u>. This Contract shall terminate one calendar year after its Effective Date unless renewed by the parties 30 days before the date it would otherwise expire.

Word Choice Issues to Think About:

"Termination." What does that mean? It will differ for each contract. What survives?

"One year." What does that mean? If it is effective June 2, 2010, does it terminate on June 2, 2011 (unless renewed)? And if so, when? At the stroke of midnight on June 1, 2011? Doesn't't resolving this issue affect both the date of termination and the deadline for renewal?

"One month." Thirty days prior? One calendar month? How to best phrase this concept? Should the drafter take the lead in suggesting the translation of the ambiguous term into something else? Issues are similar to those implicated by "One year."

Page 71–Exercise 3:

The License to use the copyrighted material shall terminate at 11:59 p.m. on the last day of each month unless:

1) the parties mutually assent to the extension of the license for another month, and

2) the Licensee pays another monthly License Fee in the amount of _____ to the Licensor before the date and time when the License would otherwise expire.

Page 71–Exercise 4:

Employment Agreement

     This employment agreement (the "Agreement") is entered into as of the _____ day of _____ , 20 ___, between Ned Armstrong (the "Employer") and _____ (the "Employee").

     The Parties agree as follows:

     Employer agrees to hire Employee, and Employee agrees to work for Employer as an advisor and counsel in Employer's financial, business, and legal matters.

     Term of Employment. This Agreement shall be in effect for one year from the date of this Agreement (the "Employment Term"). Employer shall pay Employee a salary of Fifty Thousand Dollars ($50,000.00) for the Employment Term (the "Salary"). The Salary shall be payable in twenty-four equal installments on the first and fifteenth day of each calendar month.

     Hours. Employee shall work for at least forty (40) hours each week. Employee will not receive any additional compensation for hours worked above and beyond the required forty hours.

     Leave. Employee may take up to three (3) weeks of vacation per Employment Term. Employee may take up to five (5) days off for illness per Employment Term. The Salary will continue to be paid according to schedule regardless of when vacation or sick leave is taken.

     Termination. Employer retains the right to terminate this Agreement at any time during the Employment Term. The Employer may terminate this Agreement for cause or without cause. If Employer terminates this Agreement for cause, Employee is not entitled to receive any Salary or benefits under this Agreement after the date of termination. If Employer terminates this Agreement without cause, Employee will receive all payments of Salary and benefits under this Agreement that would otherwise have been due as and when the payments would have come due. *[Editor's Comment: What is "cause". Are you intentionally leaving it undefined? If so, what authorities would you expect to use to determine its meaning in a future dispute?]*

<u>Confidentiality</u>.   Employee shall not reveal or disclose any information that Employee learns during the Employment Term about Employer's financial, business, legal, or personal matters (the "Non-Disclosure Requirement").   This Non-Disclosure Requirement shall be in effect during and after the Employment Term, regardless of whether the Employment Term expires or whether Employer causes a Termination of Employee. *[Editor's Comment: Integration clause? Other boilerplate that is desirable?]*

[Signature blocks as appropriate.]

Page 76–Exercise 1:

<u>Model Answer</u>:

     <u>Shareholders' Option to Force Purchase or Sale</u>. Either shareholder may, at any time, provide notice to the other shareholder that it is willing to buy or sell all of its or the other's shares for a stated price. Upon receipt of that notice, the other shareholder shall, within five business days, inform the shareholder triggering this procedure that the other shareholder shall purchase all of the triggering shareholder's shares or sell all of his own shares for the stated price, and failure to do so shall constitute the other shareholder's acceptance of the triggering shareholder's offer to purchase all of the other shareholder's shares for the stated price.

Page 76–Exercise 2:

Model Answer:

      A. If Buyers fail to make a payment or an interest payment or fail to perform any covenants in this Contract, Sellers may elect (1) to declare all payments and interest immediately due and (2) to terminate this Contract. Seller may terminate this Contract by giving Buyers written notice of the Seller's intent to terminate the Contract at least ninety (90) days before the termination ("Notice").

      The Notice must state:

          1) the amount due under the Contract,

          2) the time during which Buyers can make payments, and

          3) the place where Buyers can make payments.

      B. If Notice is given to Buyers at least ninety (90) days in advance of termination of this Contract by the Seller:

          1) all obligations of the Seller under this Contract are cancelled;

          2) Sellers will be reinvested with all rights and interests conveyed under this Contract;

          3) Buyers will forfeit

               (a) any payments made under this Contract ("Payments"),

          and

               (b) any rights or interest in buildings, fences, and other improvements ("Improvements");

          4) Sellers shall retain Payments and Improvements as full satisfaction of a reasonable rental for the Property and as damages sustained by Sellers; and

5) Sellers shall have the right to re-enter and take possession of the Property.

In addition to the remedies set forth in this Contract, Sellers shall have all remedies available to them at law and in equity.

Page 87–Exercise 1:

Model Answer:

A. Representation. It is intending to induce reliance. A representation speaks as of the execution of the document in which it is contained.

B. Representation and Warranty. A representation to induce reliance and a warranty because it is a promise to ensure that those facts are as stated.

C. The Statement: Representation and Warranty
    The Defense: Covenant and Indemnity
    To Pay off Liens: Covenant

D. Covenant and Guaranty. A covenant is a promise to act or not to act in the future, and the guaranty is one who promises that if another party does not perform a duty, the guarantor will.

E. Covenant and Indemnity.

F. Covenant and Indemnity.

G. Representation and Warranty.

Page 88–Exercise 2:

Model Answers:

[A]   Seller represents and warrants that, as of the date of execution of this Purchase Agreement, the Seller has, to the best of its knowledge, 750 Bamboo Fishing Rods and 1,000 Handmade Fishing Lures in inventory. The Seller represents and warrants that, as of the date of execution of this Purchase Agreement, the Seller has, to the best of its knowledge, 500 Bamboo Fishing Rods and 600 Handmade Fishing Lures in work-in-progress.

[B]   Seller represents and warrants that, as of the date of execution of this Purchase Agreement, the Seller has 900 finished Wool Sweaters in inventory and 200 Wool Sweaters in work-in-progress.
[Purchase Agreement calls for 1,000 Wool Sweaters in inventory. The Buyer relies on this representation and warranty that the inventory is "close enough," especially with 200 sweaters in progress.]

[C]   Seller represents and warrants that the Property is subject only to the liens disclosed by Seller and described in attached Exhibit A.

Seller shall indemnify and defend Buyer against all adverse claims of title not disclosed by Seller.

Seller shall pay off all liens not disclosed by Seller in this Purchase Agreement and that are deemed valid claims by the Seller or a court of law.

[D]   Mr. William Smith, the father of the Maker, shall pay the remaining principal and accrued interest due on the Note if the Maker fails to make a payment on the Note within five (5) days after the Due Date.

[E]   Mrs. Emma Jones, the mother of the Patient, shall indemnify and reimburse Patient's nurse ("Nurse") for any liabilities to third parties that (i) are caused by Patient during the time period that Patient is under Nurse's care and (ii) are paid by Nurse on behalf of Patient.

[F]   Mrs. Emma Jones ("Mother")   shall indemnify and reimburse Patient's nurse ("Nurse") for any liabilities to third parties that (i) are caused by Patient during the time period that Patient is under Nurse's care, and (ii) are paid on behalf of Patient by Nurse.

Mother shall further defend Nurse or pay Nurse's legal fees in any proceeding arising out of or related to liabilities caused by Patient while Patient is under Nurse's care.

[G]   Lessor represents and warrants that as of the day of execution of this Lease the odometer reading on the Car does not exceed 85,000 miles. Lessor represents and warrants that the 85,000-mile odometer reading on the Car is an accurate measure of the number of miles the Car has been driven.

Page 88–Exercise 3:

UCC § 2-313 Express Warranties

They are created three ways or by a combination thereof.

– First, if the seller affirms a fact about the goods and the buyer relies upon it (that is, it becomes the basis for the bargain), then an express warranty is created that the goods will conform to the affirmed fact.

– Second, the seller may offer a description of the goods during bargaining, which would create a warranty that the goods will conform to the description.

–Third, the seller may offer a sample or model of goods, which creates a warranty that the goods bought by the buyer will closely match the sample or model.

How express warranties are not created:

It is not necessary to use the specific "warranty" language, or even intend to make a warranty–a warranty may be created regardless. But, if the seller is merely stating the value of the goods or giving his own opinion or commendation of the goods, it is not a warranty, it is merely "puffing."

UCC § 2-316(1)-(3)   Disclaimer of Express Warranties

If a warranty exists, you can expressly disclaim the warranty. Express warranties and disclaimers of warranties will be construed as consistent whenever possible, but the warranty will prevail over a disclaimer if there is a conflict.

Disclaimer of Implied Warranties

To disclaim an implied warranty of merchantability, you must:

1) mention merchantability, and

2) be conspicuous if the disclaimer is in writing.

To disclaim an implied warranty of fitness, the disclaimer must:

100

1) be in writing, and

2) be conspicuous.

To impliedly disclaim an implied warranty, you must:

1) use language such as "as is" or "with all faults" or

2) have the buyer examine the goods before entering into the contract. The implied warranty no longer exists when the buyer examines the goods or had the chance to examine and refused. There is no implied warranty for defects that the buyer should have found during inspection.

The implied warranty can also be excluded if it is normal to exclude it in the trade or if during the course of dealing or course of performance on the contract, the warranty is disclaimed by either party.

Page 88–Exercise 4:

There are no warranties, express or implied, with regards to the sale of Widgets contemplated by this Purchase Agreement.

Page 88–Exercise 5:

Model Answer:

The Seller makes no warranty of merchantability for the Goods to be sold under this Purchase Agreement. The Seller makes no warranty that the Goods:

(i) will pass without objection within the trade under the contract description;

(ii) are of fair and average quality within the description;

(iii) are fit for the ordinary purposes for which the goods are used;

(iv) run of even kind, quality, and quantity within each unit and among units;

(v) are adequately packaged, contained, and labeled; and

(vi) conform to the promise or affirmations of fact made on the container or label.

[Note: Listing all of these factors from UCC § 2-314(2) that Seller disclaims may scare a Buyer away from making the deal.]

Specific example of disclaimer of merchantability:

"Seller does not warrant to Buyer that the Lumber to be sold under this Purchase Agreement is merchantable in that Seller does not warrant that the Lumber is free of termites."

Page 95-108–Exercise 1 (*Beal Bank* Letter):

[Address as per Notice Provisions and "re" line referencing loan numbers.]

Dear [Borrower]:

The FDIC has not setoff any account nor has it taken any action of any kind under either real-property-secured or personal-property-secured loans. All the FDIC has done is to freeze accounts for which there are delinquent loans outstanding. The above-referenced loans are in default and, pursuant to section __ of the loan agreements, the FDIC therefore believes that the default interest clause of the loan agreement is triggered.

The Notes that are involved here provide that "should default be made in any payment provided for in this note," a Default Rate shall be paid on any remaining balance of principal and on any remaining accrued interest. Any unpaid balance remaining under the Notes after acceleration of the Notes will accrue interest at a Default Rate of 5% per annum above the rate contracted for the Notes.

The FDIC hereby exercises the option granted to it by the Notes to accelerate the Notes and demands immediate payment of the remaining principal plus interest at the default rate.

Sincerely,

FDIC

Model Declaration of Default Letter.

[letterhead of law firm or client sending letter]

[date]

*[inside address – use
exact address in notice
provisions of contract, if any]*

        Re: Declaration of Default under *[name contract]* (the "Contract").

Dear _____:

      This firm represents *[client name]* in connection with the Contract. Under section __ of the Contract, your firm is obligated to *[specify duty breached or underlying event of default (e.g., make a quarterly payment of principal and interest within 10 days of the end of each calendar quarter)]*. Your firm has *[specify failure to perform or other event of default that has occurred]* in a timely manner as required by the contract.

      As a result, our client hereby declares a default under section __ of the Contract. Under section __ of the contract, *[specify remedies invoked]*. Therefore, *[make demand for whatever performance is now due (e.g., turnover of property, removal from job site, payment of accelerated amount, etc.)]*.

      If you have any questions or comments regarding this matter, please *[contact, call or write – consider which word you want to use]* me at the *[address, phone number, etc.]* above.

                         Very truly yours,

                         [typed name]

Page 111–Exercise 3:

Model Answer:

Your actions, as described below, constitute an event of default as described in § 9.1 of the contract. You have failed to make one month's payment within five (5) days after the date that the payment was due. Your failure to make the payment constitutes an Event of Default in § 9.1(a).

You have also recorded a mechanic's lien against the property for more than $60,000 of unpaid work done on the HVAC system. Since a mechanic's lien is neither a Senior Debt lien nor a Permitted Encumbrance as defined in the Purchase Agreement, your recording of a mechanic's lien on the property constitutes an Event of Default under § 9.1(d).

In accordance with § 9.2 of the Purchase Agreement, "upon the occurrence of an Event of Default," Lender had the option to accelerate the Note and cause it to become immediately due and payable. As the Lender, North Forty Bank hereby exercises the option to accelerate the Note and hereby declares the Note immediately due and payable under § 9.2(a) of the Purchase Agreement.

Selecting acceleration as a remedy for your default does not preclude North Forty Bank from enjoying other remedies provided to the Lender under this Purchase Agreement or by law.

Page 111–Exercise 4:

Model Answer:

Events of Default. The occurrence of any of the following events shall constitute an "Event of Default" under this Lease:

(a) any default by Tenant in the payment of rent to Landlord which is not paid within ten (10) days after the date the rent payment was due, regardless of whether or not Landlord provides Tenant with notice of the passage of the due date or the non-receipt of the rent payment by Landlord;

(b) the failure by Tenant to maintain normal business hours at the Premises within ten (10) days after Tenant receives notice of the failure to keep normal business hours from Landlord or other third party; or

(c) any use of the Premises by Tenant for a purpose other than for a retail shop in the business of selling greeting cards and other small, collectible, non-living gifts, and local crafts.

Remedies. Upon the occurrence of an Event of Default:

(a) Tenant must pay to Landlord ten percent interest on all unpaid rent, with interest compounded each month through the term of the Lease;

(b) Landlord may enter into and take possession of the Premises and all contents in and on the Premises;

(c) Landlord may sell the contents of the Premises with the proceeds serving as satisfaction for any unpaid rent or other fees, charges, or costs, and with the sale of the contents being subject only to claims by parties holding a security interest in the contents or an ownership interest in the contents; and

(d) Landlord may enter into another lease for the Premises immediately after the occurrence of an Event of Default.

All remedies of the Landlord provided in this Lease are cumulative and shall be in addition to all other rights and remedies provided by law.

Page 111–Exercise 5:

Model Answer:

Default.

After notice from Landlord of non-payment of Rent by Tenant for a period of six (6) months after the first delinquent payment, the Landlord shall be entitled to the full amount of Rent due during the six (6) month period ("Delinquent Rent") plus interest on the unpaid rent at a rate of fifteen percent, compounded monthly for each month the Delinquent Rent remains unpaid. Rent will continue to be due each month as described above.

If Landlord brings an action to remove Tenant from the Premises and the Tenant is subsequently evicted by the court proceedings, the Tenant shall pay the attorney fees and court costs of the Landlord.

If the Landlord brings an action to collect Delinquent Rent plus interest from Tenant and Landlord receives a judgment against Tenant in a court of law, Tenant must make payments according to the decree of the court. If Tenant refuses to make such payments, Landlord is entitled to hire a professional collection agent to collect on the Delinquent Rent and interest due Landlord. In addition to the amount specified by the court due Landlord from Tenant, Tenant shall pay the cost of the collection agent incurred by Landlord.

Page 111–Exercise 7:

<u>Model Answer:</u>

It is specifically agreed and understood by the parties that monetary damages would not adequately compensate the Buyer for any breach of this Purchase Agreement. Therefore, this Purchase Agreement will be specifically enforceable. The parties waive any claim or defense that there is an adequate remedy at law for a breach or threatened breach.

Page 112–Exercise 8:

<u>Model Answer:</u>

In order to avoid irreparable injury to the Premises and to the surrounding community, Tenant is in default of this Lease if it operates any business on the Premises for which the Premises is not zoned. Tenant shall not petition the city for a variance for the Premises at any time during the Term of the Lease.

Page 112–Exercise 9:

Model Answer:

Damages for breach by Seller are limited to Incidental Damages as defined in UCC § 2-715(1). Buyer may not recover consequential damages that may arise out of Seller's breach.

[I chose to limit consequential damages because they are always uncertain. Subjective determination of damages awards may get out of control in the hands of a jury. Seller would want to limit the risk of the unknown consequential damages award.]

Page 114–Exercise 1:

<u>Model Answer:</u>

[A]   <u>Counterparts</u>. This Agreement may be executed in several counterparts, each of which is an original but which together constitute one and the same document.

[B]   <u>Successors and Assigns</u>. The provisions of this Agreement will automatically extend to and be binding upon the heirs, legal representatives, successors, and assigns of the Purchaser and Author. The Purchaser is permitted to license or assign its rights under this Agreement.

<u>Plurals</u>. If more than one Author is mentioned in this Agreement or executes this Agreement, this Agreement shall be binding jointly and severally upon each of the Authors. The word "Author" as used in this Agreement shall then have a plural meaning.

<u>Transfer of Material and Rights</u>. With respect to any material and rights sold or assigned to Purchaser pursuant to this Exhibit, Author agrees to execute and deliver to Purchaser other instruments in a form satisfactory to Purchaser as it may be necessary to or desired by Purchaser for the transfer to it of the material or rights sold or assigned. The parties agree that all material and rights sold or assigned to Purchaser shall vest in the Purchaser whether or not the Author executes the necessary assignments or instruments or delivers them to Purchaser.

<u>Governing Law</u>. This Agreement is governed by the laws of the State of Georgia. The parties shall submit to any court with proper jurisdiction within the State of Georgia. The parties shall accept service of process outside the State of Georgia in any matter to be brought before a Georgia court with proper jurisdiction.

<u>Severability</u>. The provisions contained in this Agreement are severable. If any provision is found to be void or unenforceable, then the remaining provisions will continue in full force and effect and will be so construed as to give effect, as nearly as possible, to the original intent of the parties.

Entire Agreement. This Agreement contains the entire agreement between the parties. No modification will be binding upon the parties unless a writing is signed by all parties. All prior written and oral agreements are hereby revoked. The Author has not made any representations, warranties, or agreements not set forth in this Agreement.

[C]   Governing Law. This Agreement is governed by the laws of the State of South Carolina. The parties shall submit to any court with proper jurisdiction within the State of South Carolina. The parties shall accept service of process outside the State of South Carolina in any matter to be brought before a South Carolina court with proper jurisdiction.

Severability. The provisions contained in this agreement are severable. If any provision is found to be void or unenforceable, then the remaining provisions will continue in full force and effect and will be so construed as to give effect, as nearly as possible, to the original intent of the parties.

Headings. The paragraph headings used in this agreement are for convenience and reference purposes only and will in no event add to, limit, or in any manner affect the subject matter.

[D]   Waiver. A party does not waive any right under this agreement if the party fails to exercise the right or delays in exercising the right. A party who only partially exercises any rights under this Agreement shall not be precluded from further exercising the rights. If a party waives a breach of a term or condition of this Agreement, the party does not necessarily waive any other breach of the same term or condition or any other term or condition.

[E]   Events of Default. The Maker is in default of this Note if

(a) any one person comprising the Maker is in default, or

(b) any guarantor of this Note is in default.

[F]   Waivers. Maker waives any notice and demands not expressly required under this Note and Deed of Trust. A covenant, condition, right, or remedy in this Note and Deed of Trust may only be waived or modified orally if Lender specifically agrees to the oral waiver or modification in a writing. A previous waiver or failure or delay by Lender to act under the terms of this Note and Deed of Trust does not constitute a waiver for any breach of a condition or obligation within this Note and Deed of Trust.

Maker waives the right to exhaust all remedies at law or use the statute of limitations as a defense to any of the following:

(i) any demand on this Note;

(ii) any agreement to pay this Note;

(iii) any demands relating to any obligation secured by the Deed of Trust; or

(iv) any other security for this Note.

Maker expressly waives any right to withhold payment or assert as a defense against payment of any sums payable under this Note and Deed of Trust that result from liability, breach, or alleged breach of or by Lender in connection with the execution of the Purchase Agreement.

[G]   Governing Law. This Note is governed by the laws of the State of Alabama. However, when Federal law conflicts with Alabama law, Federal law applies.

Currency. All sums referred to in this Note are calculated by reference and payable in the lawful currency of the United States.

Construction. Each party and its counsel have reviewed and negotiated this Note, Deed of Trust, and other related documents at arms' length. Any ambiguities are not to be construed against either party, regardless of any rule of construction that requires ambiguities to be resolved against the drafting party.

Captions. The titles and captions used in this Note are for convenience and reference purposes only and will in no event define, limit, or modify the scope or intent of this Note.

Successors and Assigns. The provisions of this Note will extend to and be binding upon the successors and assigns of the Lender.

<u>Time</u>. Time is of the essence with regard to all terms of this Note.

[H]   <u>Severability</u>. The provisions contained in this Note are severable. If any provision is found to be invalid or unenforceable, then the remaining provisions will continue in full force and effect. A determination in one jurisdiction will have no effect on this Note unless the jurisdiction governing this Note is bound by the determination.

[I]   <u>Notices</u>. Notices and other communications ("Notices") required under this Note or required by law must be in writing and must be delivered in person; sent by FedEx or another reputable courier service for next business day delivery; sent by prepaid telex or telecopy; or deposited in the United States mail with postage prepaid, as registered or certified mail with return receipt requested. All Notices are effective when delivered in person or one (1) business day after being deposited in United States mail, even if refused, unclaimed, or undeliverable due to a change in address of which no notice was sent. The Parties may change their addresses by giving the other party fifteen (15) days written notice.

Notices to Lender must be sent to: [Lender Name]
[Lender Address]
[Lender City, State, Zip]
Attn: [Lender Contact Person]
Fax: [Lender Fax]

Copies must be sent to: [Lender's Counsel]
[Lender's Counsel's Address]
[Lender's Counsel's City, State, Zip]

Attn: [Lead Attorney]
Fax: [Lender's Counsel's Fax]

Notices to Maker must be sent to: [Maker Name]
[Maker Address]
[Maker City, State, Zip]
Attn: [Maker Contact Person]

Fax: [Maker Fax]

Copies must be sent to: [Maker's Counsel]
                                       [Maker's Counsel's Address]
                                       [Maker's Counsel's City, State,
Zip]

                               Attn: [Lead Attorney]
                               Fax: [Maker's   Counsel's
                                       Fax]

[J]   Venue. Any action brought to interpret or enforce any provision of
       this Note is to be brought in Blount County, Tennessee.

[K]   Assurances. Maker represents that it has the authority to execute this
       Note. This Note creates a valid and enforceable obligation upon
       Maker that is enforceable according to its terms.

[L]   Limitations. The relationship between Maker and Lender is that of
       borrower and lender. This Note does not imply a partnership, joint
       venture, or any other relationship between the parties. Maker does
       not have the authority to make representations, act, or incur liabilities
       on behalf of Lender. In executing this Note, Maker is not acting
       under the authority of an undisclosed principal. This Note creates no
       third-party beneficiaries.

Revised Boilerplate Assignment , Group #1, Parts A and B, p. 108:

This Special Agreement ("Agreement") is entered into and effective as of November 17, 2003 by and between Company X ("Purchaser") and Company Y ("Seller," consists of any of the terms "Seller,""Author," or "Authors."). Purchaser and Seller are collectively referred to as the "Parties," and this Agreement shall be joint and severally binding on the Parties.

(Insert Main Body of Agreement).

GENERAL PROVISIONS

A. **Entire Agreement**. This Agreement contains the entire agreement between the Parties and supercedes all prior or contemporaneous agreements, understandings, representations, warranties and statements, between the Parties with respect to the subject matter of this writing.

B. **Governing Law**. This Agreement shall be governed by California law. The Parties expressly consent to submit to the jurisdiction of any court within the state of California, and agree to accept service of process outside the State of California.

C. **Successors and Assigns**. This Agreement shall bind and inure to the benefits of the Parties and their respective heirs, legal representatives, successors and assigns, and all or any part of Purchaser's rights under this Agreement may be licensed or assigned by Purchaser to any person or entity.

D. **Counterparts**. This Agreement may be executed in any number of counterparts, each of which shall be deemed an original, and all of which shall together constitute one agreement binding upon the Parties.

E. **Cooperation**. Each party shall cooperate, take further action and shall execute and deliver such further documents as may be reasonably requested by the other party in order to carry out the provisions and purposes of this Agreement.

F. **Survivability**. If any term of the Agreement is adjudged void or unenforceable, the remaining terms or provisions of this Agreement shall remain intact and enforceable.

A.

COUNTERPARTS

All agreements between the parties constitute one binding agreement, even though all of the parties did not sign each of the individual documents.

B.

GENERAL PROVISONS

This agreement is binding on the Purchaser and Author, and all of their successors in interest. "Purchaser" is defined as the original party to this agreement and all of his successors in interest. All parties that are mentioned as an "Author" in this agreement are bound by the provisions of this Agreement. Author will deliver to Purchaser all rights and materials in a satisfactory condition. The Agreement is governed by the laws of California, and is the only binding and enforceable agreement between the parties. A written agreement between the parties is required to change a provision of the Agreement.

Boilerplate Revision Exercise

C. *No Implied Waiver.*   A party's failure to exercise a right or a party's delay in exercising a right is not a waiver of that right. A party which partially exercises a right or exercises a single right shall not be precluded from fully exercising any right or exercising any other right.

D. *Default by Maker.* Maker shall be in default upon the default of any person comprising Maker or any guarantor of this Note.

E. *Waiver and Modification.*

    1. *Waiver by Maker.* Maker waives:

        a)   All notices and demands except as expressly provided in this Note or the Deed of Trust;

        b)   Exhaustion of legal remedies;

        c)   The right to plead any statute of limitation as a defense to (i) a demand on this Note, (ii) an agreement to pay the same, (iii) a demand secured by the Deed of Trust, or (iv) any other security for this Note; and

        d)   Any right of setoff, right to withhold payment, or defense to non-payment based on the liability, breach or alleged breach of Lender in connection with the execution and delivery of the Purchase Agreement.

    2. *Written Requirement for Waiver, Modification.* Any waiver or modification of a covenant, condition, right or remedy in this Note or in the Deed of Trust must be executed by Lender in writing.

C. *Non-Waiver* – No failure of either party to strictly enforce a right under this Agreement shall be construed to constitute a waiver of the right. Also, the waiver of any party of any breach under this Agreement shall not stop the other party from later enforcing the obligation.

D. *Default* – A default by the Maker or any of its agents or any guarantors of this Note shall be deemed a default of the Maker.

E. *Waiver* – Maker waives:
- (a) all notices and demands except as expressly provided in this Note and Deed of trust;
- (b) exhaustion of legal remedies;
- (c) the right to plead any statutes of limitation as a defense to;
  - a. any demand on this Note or
  - b. any agreement to pay the same or
  - c. any demands secured by the Deed of Trust or
  - d. any other security of this Note
- (d) the right to withhold payment under this Note or Deed of Trust as a result of a breach of the Lender of the terms of the Purchase Agreement;
- (e) the right to assert breach of the Lender's liability as a defense against payment according to the terms of this Note.

Non-Waiver – The waiver of any part of this Note or Deed of Trust may be effectuated *only* by a writing signed by the Lender, and shall not constitute a waiver of any other breach or default. The waiver of the Lender of any breach of any obligation under this Note or Deed of Trust shall not repeal the obligation or stop the Lender from later enforcing the obligation.

Modification – The modification of any part of this Note or Deed of trust may be effectuated *only* by a writing signed by the Lender.

C. Waiver

1. Waiver shall not apply, or be deemed to apply, for a failure or delay in exercising any rights under this Agreement.

    a. Exercising a single or partial waiver shall not effect or waive any other rights under this Agreement

    b. Waiver of any one term or condition shall not constitute the waiver of any other term of the Agreement.

D. Constructive Default

A default by any guarantor of the Note shall create liability for the Maker of the Note.

E. Notice, Modifications and Waiver

1. **Notice.** Maker waives all notices and demands except for those provided for in the Note and Deed of Trust.

2. **Modification.** All modifications shall be in writing and executed by the Lender.

3. **Waiver.** No previous waiver, failure, or delay by the Lender shall constitute a waiver under this Note or Deed of Trust.

    a. The undersigned waives the following:
        i. exhaustion of legal remedies
        ii. the right to plead any and all statute of limitations defenses
        iii. demands secured by the Deed of Trust or this Note

    b. The Maker waives the following:
        i. any right to setoff or other withholding of payment

ii. the right to assert as a defense against payment the result of the liability, breach, or alleged breach of the Lender in connection with the execution and delivery of the Purchase Agreement.

No Implied Waiver. A waiver of a right under this contract shall NOT occur through the failure to exercise a right or a delay in exercising a right. Nor shall any single or partial exercise preclude any further exercise of such a right. Any waiver of any breach of any term of condition of this Agreement shall NOT constitute the waiver of any other breach of the same or any other term or condition.

Implied Default of the Maker. The Maker and the Guarantor of this Note shall comply with all obligations under this Agreement. In the case that either party defaults on their obligation, it will be considered a default by the Maker.

Question F.

1.   *Form of Payment.* All payments due under this Agreement shall be made in the lawful currency of the United States.

2.   *Construction of Document.* Maker and Lender have reviewed and negotiated this Note, Deed of Trust, and all other documents executed with this Note at arms length and the Parties have had the opportunity to seek the assistance of legal counsel. The Parties agree that this Note shall not be construed against the drafting party.

3.   *Titles and Captions.* The titles and captions in this Note are inserted only for convenience and do not modify the terms of this Note.

4.   *Assignment.* The term Lender, as used in this Note, shall apply to any successor or assignee of Lender.

*Note: The "time is of the essence" provision seems unnecessary.

Question G.

Unenforceable Provisions. Even though a provision of this Note is declared invalid or unenforceable by a court of competent jurisdiction, the remainder of this Note shall be valid and enforceable. A provision that is declared invalid or unenforceable in one jurisdiction shall still be valid and enforceable in all other jurisdictions.

Question H.

Section H

Communications Between Parties.

H.1   *Method of Delivery.* In the event that one party must send notice, demand, request, or other communication (the "communication") to the other party, the communication shall be delivered:

1.   in person;
2.   through Federal Express, or any other reliable source, for next business day delivery;
3.   by prepaid telephone, telex, or telecopy; or

4. by depositing in the United States mail, postage prepaid, registered or certified mail, return receipt requested.

H.2 *Effect on Receiving Party*. All communications shall be effective upon personal delivery or one business day after being delivered pursuant to Section H.1(2) through (4). A party shall be deemed to have received the communication if it rejects or refuses to accept the communication, or the communication cannot be delivered because of a changed address and no notice was given of the change, as proscribed below.

H.3 *Addresses/Change of Address*. The Parties shall use the addresses listed below, but any party, upon 15 days prior written notice, has the right to change its address to any address in the United States of America.

If to Lender:	If to Maker:
[Lender's Address]	[Maker's Name]
[Lender Address]	[Maker Address]
[Lender City, State, Zip]	[Maker City, State, Zip]
Attn: [Lender contact person]	Attn: [Maker contact person]
Fax: [Lender Fax]	Fax: [Maker Fax]

With Copies to: With Copies to:
[Lender's Counsel]   [Maker's Counsel]
[Lender's Counsel Address]   [Maker's Counsel Address]
[Lender's Counsel City, State, Zip]   [Maker's Counsel City, State, Zip]
Attn: [Lead Attorney] Attn: [Lead Attorney]
Fax: [Lender's Counsel Fax] Fax: [Maker's Counsel Fax]

K Drafting
Boilerplate Assignment-page 107
November 15, 2003

F. Purchase Money Promissory Note

1. *Lawful Money.* All payments shall be paid with the lawful currency of the United States.
2. *Assistance of Legal Counsel.* Maker and Lender are able to seek legal counsel.
3. *Construing Against Drafter.* Nothing contained in this Note, or any documents in connection with this Note, shall be construed against either party. This applies regardless of which party drafts the document.
4. *Headings.* The titles and captions in this Note do not bind the scope or intent of this Note. Titles and captions are for convenience purposes.
5. *Successors or Assigns.* This Note is binding on the Lender as well as the Lender's successors or assigns.
7. *Time of Essence.* Time is of the essence of this Note and any other documents in connection with this Note.

G. Enforceability of Promissory Note

1. *Validity or Enforceability.* If any provision of this Note is declared invalid or unenforceable by a court of competent jurisdiction, the declaration shall not affect the remaining provisions.
2. *Multiple Jurisdictions.* The decision of one jurisdiction shall not affect the enforceability of any provision of this Note in another jurisdiction.

H. Communications Between Parties

1. *Writings.* All communications between the Parties shall be in writing.
2. *Who can make Delivery.* Delivery shall be made by a representative of the Party sending communication; Federal Express; or another reputable courier.
3. *Methods of Delivery.* Delivery of communications shall be made in the following ways:
   a. next business day delivery;
   b. prepaid telephone, telex, or telecopy; OR
   c. United States mail, postage prepaid, registered, or certified mail
4. *Notice.* Notice shall be effective if personally delivered, or one (1) business day after being deposited in the United States mail. If no notice is given by the receiving party that it refuses or rejects the delivery or that

it changed its address does not affect the notice by the party sending the communication. If fifteen (15) days prior written notice is given, the parties shall have the right to change its addresses:

If to Lender:	[Lender Name] [Lender Address] [Lender City, State, Zip] Attn: [Lender contact person] Fax: [Fax]
With copies to:	[Lenders Counsel] [Lender Counsels Address] [Lender counsel City, State, Zip] Attn: [Lead Attorney] Fax: [Fax]
If to Maker:	[Maker Name] [Maker Address] [Maker City, State, Zip] Attn: [Maker contact person] Fax: [Fax]
With copies to:	[Makers Counsel] [Makers Counsels Address] [Maker counsel City, State, Zip] Attn: [Lead Attorney] Fax: [Fax]

Charlotte Haynes
11-17-03
pg.108: F, G, H

F.
PAYMENTS

All sums referred to in this document shall be payable in United States Currency.

CONSTRUCTION OF THIS NOTE, DEED OF TRUST AND OTHER CONNECTED DOCUMENTS

ASSUMPTION: "this Note, Deed of Trust and other documents executed in connection with this Note" have already been defined in the definitions section as "Transaction Documents."

Both the Maker and the Lender, with the assistance of counsel, have reviewed and negotiated the Transaction Documents. Thus, the Transaction Documents shall not be strictly construed against either party regardless of who drafted the document.

EFFECT OF TITLES AND CAPTIONS

The titles and captions in this Note are inserted for convenience only and shall not be considered or referred to in resolving questions of interpretation or construction of any Transaction Document.

INCLUSION OF SUCCESSORS AND ASSIGNEES

Any reference to the Lender in this Note shall include any of the Lender's successors or assignees.

G.

SEVERABILITY

If any provision of this Note is declared unenforceable, the remaining provisions of this Note shall remain in full effect.

EFFECT OF UNENFORCEABILITY ON OTHER JURISDICTIONS

If any provision of this Note is declared unenforceable in one jurisdiction it may still be enforceable under the laws of another jurisdiction.

H.
Section 1
COMMUNICATIONS

1.1 Forms of Communications

All communications from one party to another required by this document or by law
("Communication") shall be completed by:

   i.   hand delivery to the intended addressee,

   ii.   depositing the Communication with Federal Express or another reputable private courier service for next day delivery,

   iii.   depositing the Communication in the United States mail with adequate postage prepaid,

   iv.   sending the Communication by registered or certified mail, return receipt requested, or

   v.   sending the Communication by prepaid telephone, telex, or telecopy to the intended addressee.

All written communication shall be given directly to the intended addressee, addressed to the intended addressee at the address or contact number provided below in section 1.5, or to any other address or contact number that the intended addressee designates according to section 1.4.

1.2 Effective delivery dates of Communications

The effective dates of the delivery of a Communication are listed below under their respective method of delivery.

   i.   **Personal Delivery.** Delivery made by this method shall be effective on the date of that delivery.

   ii.   **United States Mail.** Delivery made by this method shall be effective one (1) business day after being deposited.

iii. **Other Methods.** Delivery made by any other method designated in section 1.1 shall be effective on the date the Communication is deposited to the courier or postal employee, or upon its successful transmission by prepaid telephone, telex, or telecopy.

1.3 Refusal of delivery

Addressee's refusal of delivery or the inability to deliver because the intended addressee failed to change its address as provided below in section 1.4, shall be deemed an effective delivery on a date consistent with section 1.2 above.

1.4 Change of Address

Either party ("Changing Party") shall have the right to change its address at any time provided that:

i. the Changing Party gives written notice to the other party and its counsel at least fifteen (15) days in advance of the address change, and

ii. the new address is within the United States of America.

1.5 <u>List of Current Addresses</u>

If to Lender: [Lender's Name]
                       [Address]
                       Attn: [Lender contact person]
                       Fax: [Fax]

With copies to: [Lender's Counsel]
                       [Address]
                       Attn: [Lead Attorney]
                       Fax: [Fax]

If to Maker: [Maker's Name]
                       [Maker's Address]
                       Attn: [Maker contact person]
                       Fax: [Fax]

With copies to: [Maker's Counsel]
[Address]
Attn: [Lead Attorney]
Fax: [Fax]

I. **Choice of Forum.** The parties shall litigate disputes to this agreement exclusively in
   courts venued in Cook County, Illinois.

J. **Maker's Representations.** The Maker represents the following:
   J.1. Maker has the full power and authority to execute and deliver this Note.

   J.2. This Note constitutes a binding obligation of the Maker.

K.1. **Relationship between the Parties.**
   K.1.1. The only relationship between Maker and Lender is that of borrower and lender. Maker and Lender are not partners in any meaning of the word.

   K.1.2. Maker shall have no right to act on the Lender's behalf.

K.2. **No Third-Party Beneficiaries.** The Maker represents the following:
   K.2.1. Maker executes this Note on its own behalf and not as an agent of an undisclosed principal.

   K.2.2. No third-party beneficiary shall exist because the Maker executes this Note.

I.   **Venue.** The exclusive venue of any action brought to interpret or enforce the provisions of this Note shall be in Cook County, Illinois.

J.   **Maker's Representations.** Maker represents the following:

1. maker has the full power and authority to execute and deliver this Note,

2. this Note constitutes the valid and binding obligation of Maker, and

3. this Note is enforceable in accordance with its terms.

K.   **Relationship Between Maker and Lender.** The Relationship between Maker and Lender is that of borrower and lender respectively, and no partnership, joint venture, or other similar relationship shall be inferred from this Note. Maker shall have no right or authority to make representations, act, or incur debts or liabilities on behalf of Lender.

L.   **This Note and Third Parties.** Maker is not executing this Note as an agent or nominee for an undisclosed principle, and no third-party beneficiaries are or shall be created by the execution of this Note.

I.   **Governing Jurisdiction**. The parties shall bring legal or equitable actions concerning this Note must be brought in Cook County, Illinois.

J.   **Maker's Authority**. Make represents that it has the express authority to execute and deliver this Note.

    Obligations Binding. Maker represents that this Note binds the Maker to perform the obligations of this Note.

K.   **Nature of Relationship Between the Parties**. The legal relationship between the parties to this Note is Borrower and Lender. Neither Party to this Note shall have the right to act on behalf of the other Party in any manner, unless otherwise expressly provided. No third party beneficiaries shall be created by this Note, unless otherwise expressly provided.

Lease Provision

A. In order to avoid irreparable injury to the Premises and the surrounding community, Tenant is in default of this lease if it operates any business on the Premises for which the premises is not zoned. Tenant shall not petition the city for a variance for the Premises at any time during the Term of the Lease. (56 words)

B. Tenant acknowledges and agrees that (i) the Premises is currently zoned for residential use and (ii) operation of any business on the Premises will create discord and decrease property values thereby causing irreparable injury to the Premises and the surrounding community. Tenant agrees that it will neither (a) conduct a business on the Premises nor (b) petition the city for a variance for the Premises. Tenant further agrees that a breach of the preceding covenant shall be a default under the Lease entitling Landlord to (x) obtain a preliminary injunction or restraining order, (y) immediately terminate the Lease, and (z) any other remedies available at law or in equity. (109 words)

C. Tenant acknowledges and agrees that (i) the Premises is currently zoned for residential use and (ii) operation of any business on the Premises will create discord and decrease property values thereby causing irreparable injury to the Premises and the surrounding community .It shall be a material violation of the terms of this Lease for Tenant to (a) conduct a business on the Premises or (b) petition the city for a variance for the Premises. (74 words)

Page 118–Exercise 4:

Model Answer:

If the Service Fee is found unenforceable or void because it is excessive, usurious, or a forfeiture, the Parties expressly agree that the price of the Property shall then be increased by 0.1% in order to compensate the Seller for the non-receipt of the Service Fee.

Page 118–Exercise 5:

Model Answer:

<u>Governing Law</u>.   This Lease is governed by the laws of the State of Tennessee.

Page 118–Exercise 6:

Model Answer:

Any action brought by either Party to interpret or enforce any provision of this Note and seeking injunctive or other equitable relief is to be brought in Hamilton County, Tennessee.

Any action brought by either Party to interpret or enforce any provision of this Note and seeking monetary damages is to be brought in any court with proper jurisdiction over the matter in the State of Tennessee.

Page 118–Exercise 7:

Note: The key to which clause to choose depends on the bargaining power of the parties.

In a case where one party has more bargaining power and leverage than the other (and this party will often be the drafting party, such as a form lease or purchase agreement), inconsistencies should be construed against the party with more leverage and control over the document:

Model Answer #1:

"Any inconsistencies or ambiguities within this Lease are to be resolved against the drafting party."

Model Answer #2:

In a case where the parties are on equal footing and the document has been fully negotiated, inconsistencies must not be construed against either party outright. The matter should be brought before a neutral party (i.e., court, arbiter, mediator, etc.):

"The parties, together with their counsel, have reviewed and negotiated this Purchase Agreement, and the parties agree not to apply to this Purchase Agreement the rule of construction that ambiguities and inconsistencies are to be resolved against the drafting party."

Page 124–Exercise 1:

Model Answer:

Arbitration. Disputes arising out of this Agreement are to be subject to arbitration only when one party submits written notice to the other party a demand for arbitration. If no notice is given within sixty (60) days after the dispute arises, the dispute will be submitted to a court of law.

When the notice of a demand for arbitration is received by the other party, the non-demanding party has ten (10) days to select the forum for the arbitration and to notify the other party in writing of the forum selection.

After forum selection, each party has thirty (30) days to select an arbiter of their choice but who is a member of the American Arbitration Association. The two arbiters shall then appoint a third arbiter, also a member of the American Arbitration Association, within a reasonable time.

Procedural Rules. Each party may present its case to the panel of three arbiters. The non-demanding party may choose to present its case first or last. Since the decision by the arbiters is not binding on the parties and may be appealed to a court of law (see below), there will be no discovery or disclosure of facts required. The rules of evidence do not apply. After presentation of the cases, the panel of arbiters will decide the case, with the neutral arbiter issuing the opinion for the panel. The parties may not challenge the arbiters' ruling. The arbiters' opinion is advisory. Either party may submit the dispute to a court of law but only after the arbiters have issued their opinion.

Page 124–Exercise 2:

<u>Model Answer:</u>

<u>Mediation</u>. Disputes arising out of this Agreement are to be subject to mediation before the dispute may be brought before a court of law. When a dispute arises, the aggrieved party must notify the other party in writing of the dispute and that this mediation clause has been triggered.

<u>Procedure</u>. The attorneys for the parties must agree on a mediator within thirty (30) days after the mediation notice is sent. The mediator will select the date and place that the mediation will occur. The parties will each present their case to the mediator outside the presence of the other party. The mediator will then suggest a solution to each party and act as a liaison between the parties as they negotiate an agreement.

Either party may choose to cease the mediation at any time after the mediator has heard both sides and presented at least one solution. If a party chooses to cease mediation, the dispute must be brought before a court of law.

If both parties agree to a solution proposed during mediation, the parties must sign a written statement outlining the agreed upon solution. The written signed statement makes the mediation decision binding upon the parties and precludes the parties from bringing this dispute before a court of law.

If one party refuses to abide by the mediation agreement, the other party may bring the case before a court of law to request enforcement of the mediation agreement.

Page 124—Exercise 3:

<u>Model Answer:</u>

Any action brought to interpret or to enforce any provisions of this Lease is to be brought in any court with proper jurisdiction in the State of Montana. The parties expressly waive the right to a trial by jury.

Page 124 –Exercise 4:

This is obviously a very open ended discussion question, but it is very important as so much of ethics discussion in law school tends to focus on litigation rather than transactional practice. Here are some thoughts on the issue from Professor Carl Pierce:

> Breach of Contractual Obligations and Other Duties of Contracting Parties
>
> Professor Hazard specifically exempted breach of contract from the misconduct he thought lawyers should not be allowed to encourage or assist.[8] Although not without some doubts, I concur with his judgment because the law in such cases is a law that for the most part is created by the parties, rather than the state. It is also commonly said that the purpose of contract law is not to deter the breach, but only to require the breaching party to internalize the costs of the breach, e.g., the loss to the other of the benefit of the bargain, so that the breach will be economically efficient.[9] Some might even argue that efficient breach is preferable to inefficient performance.
>
> Another way to think about the difference between contract and tort is that contract should be viewed as a set of alternative promises, e.g., I will either perform as promised or compensate you for your loss of benefit in such amount agreed to by us or determined by a court. It is not wrongful to elect the latter option. One can also find support for a distinction between engaging in tortious conduct and breaching contracts in that punitive damages are not generally available for a breach of contract not involving an independent tort."[10] While this is not the place for a full evaluation of the theory underlying the enforcement of contracts,

8 440. Hazard, *supra* note 46, at 682B83.

9 441. See E.ALLENFARNSWORTH,CONTRACTS, § 12.3 (3d ed. 1999).

10 *See* JOHN D. CALAMARI & JOSEPH M. PERILLO, THE LAW OF CONThACTS 542—43 (4th ed. 1998).

such theory evidences that there is not a sufficient legal consensus that breaching a contract is sufficiently wrongful to justify depriving clients of the privilege of having a lawyer assist them with such a breach. As noted, however, such a straightforward breach of contract must, of course, be distinguished from a breach of contract involving misrepresentation about or concealment of the breach. That's a fraud a lawyer must not encourage or assist.

In spite of this general exception for breach of contract, there are three special situations that merit mention. The first relates to the inclusion in a contract of a clause that the lawyer knows is unenforceable as a matter of law, either because it is expressly prohibited by statute or has been held to be either unconscionable or contrary to public policy. The second relates to the mandatory obligation of good faith and fair dealing that is implied, as a matter of law, in every contract. The third relates to public policy exceptions to the right under contract law of an employer to discharge an employee without cause or, as some would say, even for a bad cause.

The first issue relates to the formation of contracts. It was first considered by the ABA when the Kutak Commission proposed a prohibition against a lawyer counseling or assisting a client "in the preparation of a written instrument containing terms the lawyer knows are expressly prohibited by law."[11] The ABA House

---

[11] MODEL RULES OF PROF'L CONDUCT R. 1.2(d) (Commission Proposal Rule 1983), *reprinted in* ABA, THE LEGISLATIVE HISTORY OF THE MODEL RULES OF PROFESSIONAL CONDUCT 31B33 (1987). A prior draft more broadly, and perhaps ambiguously, prohibited a lawyer from counseling or assisting a client "in the preparation *of* a written instrument containing terms the lawyer knows or reasonably should know are legally prohibited." MODEL RULES OF PROF'L CONDUCT R. 1.2(d) (Official Draft 1981), as *reprinted in* STEPHEN GILLERS & ROY D. SIMON, REGULATION OF LAWYERS: STATUTES AND STANDARDS *35* (2003). A still earlier draft provided that "a lawyer shall not conclude an agreement, or assist a client in concluding an agreement,

of Delegates did not approve this addition to Rule 1 .2(d).[12] New Jersey's Rule 1.2(d), however, contains such a prohibition,[13] but it stands alone among the states. The question is whether the Kutak Commission and New Jersey have the right idea. I think they do because to knowingly include in a contract a term expressly prohibited by law is to flaunt or show contempt for the law in a way I cannot distinguish from the commission of a crime, a violation of a statutory prohibition, the perpetration of a fraud, or engaging in intentionally tortious conduct. The only problem I have with the Kutak Commission proposal and the New Jersey rule is that they may be too narrow and, at the same time, ambiguous. Both problems arise from the specification that the term must be "expressly prohibited by law." Considering the alternative formulations that were considered prior to the Kutak Commission settling on its proposal to the House of Delegates, I would add a prohibition against counseling or assisting a client in conduct the lawyer knows "involves the inclusion in a contract of a provision, the inclusion of which has been prohibited by statute or regulation or which has been held by the [state's highest court], to be contrary to public policy, unconscionable, or otherwise unenforceable as a matter of law." My only

---

that the lawyer knows or reasonably should know is illegal, contains legally prohibited terms, would work a fraud, or would be held to be unconscionable as a matter of law." William T. Vukowich, *Lawyers and the Standard Form Contract System: A Model Rule That Should Have Been,* 6 Geo. J. Legal Ethics 799, 833 (1993)

(citing MODEL RULES DISCUSSION DRAFT RULE 4.3).

[12] MODEL RULES OF PROF'L CONDUCT R. 1.2(d) (Commission Proposal Rule 1983), *reprinted in* ABA, THE LEGISLATIVE HISTORY OF THE MODEL
RULES OF PROFESSIONAL CONDUCT 3 1—33 (1987).

[13] N.J. RULES OF PROF'L CONDUCT R. 1.2(d) (2004) (stating that a lawyer shall not assist a client "in the preparation of a written instrument containing
terms the lawyer knows are expressly prohibited by law").

reservation with respect to this proposal is whether it is necessary. As Hazard and Hodes have noted, to include such a clause in a contract could be viewed as fraudulent if it is likely to mislead customers as to their rights."[14] I would see it as a representation of the client's opinion that the clause was enforceable, which would imply an assertion that the client did not know facts incompatible with the opinion or that the client knew of some facts that would support the opinion. If the client knew that the clause or contract was unenforceable, such a representation would be fraudulent, and Rule 1.2(d) would apply anyway. I would, however, prefer to give lawyers more guidance about their responsibilities, particularly when the guidance reinforces the basic proposition that lawyers, of all persons, must not allow their services to be used in knowing violation of the law.

The second issue involves the question of whether a lawyer should be allowed to assist a client in conduct that would violate the client's contractual obligation of good faith and fair dealing. I single out this issue because this obligation is imposed as a matter of law on all persons who enter in contractual relations with others.[15] It is also a duty that the parties are not free to eliminate.[16] Also, it parallels the duty of good faith expected of fiduciaries.[17] In the end, however, I have concluded that the duty of good faith and fair dealing in contracts differs from other legal duties because a person cannot be subject to liability for breach of such a duty. It serves only as justification for terminating the contractual rights of the party who has acted in

---

[14] HAZARD & HODES, *supra* note *51, § 5.12,* illustration 5-13 (2003).

[15] 447 U.C.C. § 1-203 (2004).

[16] *Id.*

[17] *See, e.g.,* ABA MODEL BUSINESS CORPORATION ACT § 8.30 (2004) ("Each member of the board of directors, when discharging the duties of a director shall act . . . in good faith).

bad faith. Also, because the doctrine of good faith "merely directs a court towards interpreting contracts within the commercial context in which they are created, performed and enforced,"[18] this duty would appear to be nothing more than an extension of the parties agreement that should not be treated differently from other provisions that might be breached and would both justify the other parties nonperformance and subject the breaching party to liability for breach of contract. Thus I would not propose precluding lawyers from assisting a client in the breach of a contractual duty of good faith or fair dealing.

Carl A Pierce, Client Misconduct in the 21st century, 35 U. Memphis L. Rev. 731, 900-903 (2005) (used by permission).

---

18 U.C.C. 1-203.

V.   Notes Relating to the Appendices
The following are edited composite student analysis of the documents in the appendices.

APPENDIX 1 - PROMISSORY NOTE

- The title should be underlined but it does use a generic term to describe the type of contract being contemplated.
- The first paragraph identifies the parties and the type of transaction they are documenting and establishes defined terms for the parties. It appears that there is no other "recital."
- This Promissory Note jumps right into what looks like "defined terms" and there is no heading.
    - In this case the document is a rather short one and the definitions are introduced early but they are not labeled as such.
    - Defined terms simplify references to longer, more detailed concepts, people, places, and things.
- INTEREST
    - This section could be more well defined and numbered or lettered to allow the reader to more easily find the term and should be numbered or lettered because of proper form usage.
    - The use of the word "hereof" should be eliminated altogether or replaced with a more "plain English" word.
    - The drafter uses redundant language. The draft should simply say in regard to the Reference Rate, "the interest rate charged during each month shall be based on the Reference Rate in effect on the first day of each successive month and shall continue to do so throughout the life of the Note."
- TIME AND FORM OF PAYMENT
    - This should be more well marked on the draft.
    - What does legal holiday mean?
        - Is the drafter referring to Federal legal holidays or state ones too.
        - What does the drafter mean when he says "interest shall be payable thereon during such extensions."
            - The word "thereon" should be eliminated because it is confusing and not plain English.
            - If the due date falls on a Saturday, Sunday, or legal holiday that is not the same as a typical extension when it is paid on the next business day.
            - If the due date falls on a Saturday and there is a legal holiday on the following Monday is the drafter contemplating a three day extension in which interest will accrue?
- EVENT OF DEFAULT

- This should be more clearly identifiable.
- What does the drafter mean by "any other default or event of default occurs hereunder?"
  - Hereunder is not plain English and should be eliminated.
  - What events is the drafter contemplating and what are other defaults.
    - Perhaps a list should be incorporated to identify the types of things that the drafter is referring to.
- Is the mention of instrument, document, and agreement between Maker and Payee an inclusive list?
- The payee may, at its option, at any time thereafter, declare the entire unpaid principal balance of this Note plus all accrued Interest to be immediately due and payable, without notice or demand.
  - What if there was an honest mistake by no fault of their own?
  - There is no option to cure the default?
  - Is this even legal?
    - Many default provisions include the concept of a right to cure, or fix, the default and avoid application of the remedies provided in the contract.
    - If default occurs, notice of the default should be drafted in unequivocal language.
    - Both state and federal courts have made it clear the unquestionable principal that, even when the terms of a note do not require notice or demand as a prerequisite to accelerating a note, the holder must take affirmative action to notify the debtor that it intends to accelerate. *Green v. Carlstrom.*
    - A party having an option to declare a note due and payable cannot simply by his own secret intention, never disclose by act or words, claim that he declared the note due and payable. *Trigg v. Arnott.*
      - It appears that even though the Note clearly states that notice does not have to be given, notice of some kind must by communicated before the Note is due and payable.
  - Liquidated damages in the amount of 5% of the installment not paid can be very small.
    - If the majority of the installment was paid, 5% of the portion not paid might not be enough to cover expenses for administering default.

- Perhaps a hard figure should be inserted here with a percentage.
  - The language should read something to the effect that the maker agrees to pay immediately to payee as liquidated damages an amount equal to 5% of the installment not paid or $500,000 whichever is the greater number.
  - How long can they delay before it is an actual waiver of their rights under the contract? Can they fail to exercise their rights under this contract indefinitely?
  - Maybe a hard number should be used instead of such a broad word.
- APPLICATION OF PAYMENTS
  - What are costs and fees.
    - I would like to see exactly what are the costs and the fees.
    - What does it mean that the payee shall have the continuing and exclusive right to apply or reverse and reapply payments. A more plain English statement might be necessary.
  - I would insert "reasonable" into "Maker will pay all cost and expenses including, without limitation, attorney fees." It is probably there, but best to be explicit.
  - Are the maker's waivers inclusive?
- SEVERABILITY
  - Good boiler plate language
  - What does it mean when the drafter rights "shall be governed by and construed in accordance with the internal laws as opposed to the conflicts of law provisions?"
    - If the drafter has to put in language such as "as opposed to" then that signals to me that it is not well written.
    - It should be able to be simply said in plain English and not compared to another set of laws in order to figure out what the drafter means by "internal laws."
  - The maker has to submit to a certain forum and then has to say that he will not challenge the forum as inconvenient. This is redundant.
- WAIVER OF JURY TRIAL
  - Can the maker ever have a right to a jury because he seems to waive his right in "any present or future instrument or agreement between payee and maker." Does this clause run to all other agreements in the future that have not even been contemplated?

- The use of all capitalization does not make it easier for me to read.
- The use of all capitalization and bold face makes me think something is wrong with the document and just makes it look "weird."
- An easier way to make it strand out is just to put a heading on it in bold and underlined and maybe increase the font size.

APPENDIX 2 – ASSET PURCHASE AND SALE AGREEMENT

- The title should be underlined.
  - A transactional document memorializes the deal. The transactional documents are intended to capture the agreements of the parties, and their respective rights and obligations and to establish a set of rules that will govern future dealings.
- There is an introductory paragraph and it is well written and in the proper form.
  - The introductory paragraph identifies the parties and the type of transaction they are documenting.
    - It establishes defined terms for the parties. Using defined terms for the parties means that they will not come up again until the signature block.
    - It provides a reference date for the document.
- RECITALS
  - Preambles or recitals set the context for the agreement and are useful in later interpretations.
  - They provide a place to list relevant transactional documents and other things.
  - The recitals should be written in plain English.
  - They should be preceded by a capital letter "numbering" or "ordinal" system.
  - Facts should be included in the recitals that help the reader grasp the nature, purpose, and basis for the agreement.
    - The relationship and goals of the parties.
    - The nature of the transaction.
    - Other transactional documents.
  - Unnecessary facts should not be included and care should be taken to be accurate.
    - It is good practice to be more general then specific in the recitals and to not recite everything.
    - Facts used in the recitals may be used later in litigation to prove which they state.
  - The recitals in this draft could be construed as the "real" agreement because they are stated prior to the section of the document labeled the "agreement."
    - The accuracy of the recitals should be addressed in the "real" agreement.
    - A provision should be included that says the parties represent and warrant to one another that the recitals

are accurate, perhaps with a "to the best of their knowledge" limitation.

- One or both of the parties may want to disclaim any implication that they are representing or warranting that the recitals are accurate.
- A provision regarding the accuracy of the recitals should be expressed clearly in the main "agreement" section of the document to avoid any implication that the recitals are not part of the agreement. The parties included such a statement which makes the recitals part of the agreement and enforceable.

- It is good to have the background information regarding where the contract was entered into because it could have an impact on the laws that will be used for interpretation or enforcement of the contract.
- ARTICLE I – SALE AND PURCHASE
  - The Seller decided to list the assets that are excluded from sale.
    - It is important to make the list exhaustive of excluded assets because if you do not list an asset then it is considered as part of the Buyers purchase.
      - The list only includes those assets that are excluded not those assets that the Buyer is going to purchase so it is important to take care in preparing the list of excluded assets because if they are not excluded specifically then they are part of the Sale Agreement.
  - The Seller probably has a vehicle that is being offered as part of the Sale Agreement and this vehicle probably has an outstanding loan on it.
    - The Seller will purchase both the vehicle and the outstanding loan as opposed to purchasing the vehicle and then having the Seller pay off the outstanding loan.
    - It is also important to free-up any and all assets that have use restrictions placed on them if this can be done before the closing of the sale.
  - It is important not to commingle funds.

- The Seller does not want to commingle funds that are rightfully his with funds that, according to the Sale Agreement, do not belong to him. The funds are not the property of the Seller and therefore can not be considered as part of his working capital.
  - I would recommend that the deposit be larger than the Specified Liquidated damages or at least equal to it.
    - It is important that the Seller protect himself at all stages of this complicated deal in the event that the Buyer does not perform his obligations under the Sale Agreement.
  - The letter of credit should be high enough to cover the loan and interest payments throughout the life of the loan in the event that the Buyer defaults and the Note is called due.
    - A letter of credit is good because it is "clean" and easy to gauge the financial health of the Buyer and is incumbent on the bank to periodically check the financial position of the Buyer.
    - The Buyer needs a replacement letter of credit to be in effect at all times until the Seller has received payment of all amounts payable pursuant to the Note. I would include language that gives the Seller the ability to request a letter of credit at any time if he has reason to believe that the Buyer is having financial hardships.
- ARTICLE TWO – ESCROW
  - Defined terms are introduced "on the fly" and it makes the document much easier to read and understand.
  - The duties of the escrow agent are defined and outlined.
  - In the event that the close of Escrow has not occurred the Seller shall return to the Buyer the Deposit, minus the amount of Seller's attorneys' fees and any other costs incurred in connection with the transaction.
    - The Agreement then goes on to read, however, the total amount of such fees and costs shall not exceed in the aggregate X amount of dollars.
      - If there is a limit on the amount of fees that the Seller can receive then there is no need for the first part of the clause.
        - The Agreement should just say that the Seller will get this amount of

money in the event the Escrow does not close.

- o A letter of credit is a good guarantee from a financial institution and it is good to keep the letter current with the initial Note plus interest payments that were loaned at the time of the signing of the Note.
- o It is important to have an escrow agency handle the arrangements because they are a neutral third party with no conflicts of interests.
    - ▪ It is important to anticipate problems and if a problem does arise it is necessary to have a neutral third party that is handling the arrangements so there is no sense of bias or unfair treatment.
- ARTICLE THREE – CONDITIONS TO THE PARTIES OBLIGATIONS
    - o The conditions apparently cannot be waived but both the Buyer and the Seller have certain conditions that they must meet in order for the Sale Agreement to close.
    - o It does not appear that there are any representations or warranties because the language does not specify that they are as such.
        - ▪ A covenant is a promise to act or not to act in the future.
            - • Covenants are generally drafted in the form of a "shall clause."
            - • The word "shall" is not used in this clause.
        - ▪ It appears that such clauses are a "promise" if anything.
- ARTICLE FOUR – BUYER'S DELIVERIES
    - o The buyer must deliver the balance of the payment due at the close of escrow in order for the sale to be final.
    - o The obligations of the Buyer is to deliver cash or cash equivalent.
- ARTICLE FIVE – SELLER'S DELIVERIES TO ESCROW AGENT
    - o It is important to have all the documents agreed to upfront to prevent delay and to prevent the sale from failing at the close of Escrow.
        - ▪ If a particular deal is never going to be completed or has varying obstacles in order for it to be completed, it is important to know what those

- problems are as soon as possible so as to limit time, expenses and frustration.
  - It is important to agree on all the documents up front before closing because you never know what can be hidden among the documents.
    - Attention to detail is imperative.
  - o It is important to have all deeds and titles free of all encumbrances and/or claims of ownership from third parties.
  - o Sometimes it can be hard to find or gain access to original documents for a variety of reasons and it is important to know this before buying any asset.
    - An asset could be absolutely useless and worthless without the proper documentation, such as a vehicle, because the vehicle will not be able to be title and it will not be able to be resold.
      - The vehicle in essence becomes a liability.
- ARTICLE SIX – BUYERS REPRESENTATIONS
  - o This section should not be all capitalized.
    - It is more difficult to read and does not make it stand out as the drafter was probably intending it to.
    - The length of the clause is too long to use capitalization throughout the entirety.
  - o I find it hard to believe that the Seller can contract out of having any liability in regard to potentially hazardous material located on the real property that he is now selling to the Buyer who apparently assumes all liability.
    - What if the Buyer becomes insolvent and hazardous waste is found on the real property is it this contracts intention to bring the Sellers liability for that hazardous material down to zero?
      - The EPA will in no uncertain terms go after any person who has money for the clean up that has or had any connection to the real property that is hazardous.
        - o Can you really contract out of a hazardous waste site and push that problem on to another person?
- ARTICLE SEVEN – PRORATIONS, FEES, AND COSTS
- ARTICLE EIGHT – RECORDATION: DISTRIBUTION OF FUNDS AND DOCUMENTS

- o All documents are handled, organized, and recorded by the escrow agent which is good practice.
- ARTICLE NINE – DEFAULT
  - o The wording of section 9.1 should be changed.
    - There should be just a final number listed that shows what the Seller is entitled to in the event the Buyer defaults.
      - There is no need to write out why the Seller is entitled to such monies in the event of a default.
      - This section should also not be capitalized.
      - It also is spaced rather interestingly.
        - o Almost one full page is ignored (is it the way my printer printed out the pages?).
        - o There is a space for both the Buyer's and Seller's initials as if it is a contract within a contract.
- ARTICLE TEN – GENERAL PROVISIONS
  - o Good use of boiler plate language and terms.
  - o The contract is applicable in one particular state which should be inserted right into the Agreement.
    - The contract also mentions federal laws and choice of laws provisions which are concerned when both federal laws and state laws speak to the same issue and/or looks to other bodies of law for guidance.
  - o The Seller is fortunate enough to be allowed to entertain other offers while he negotiates the present Agreement.
    - The Seller benefits enormously from this because he has a "back-up" in the event the deal does not go through.
      - The Seller could be motivated to try and back out of the present deal if he get a substantially better offer.
      - The Seller could just become "difficult" to work with until the Buyer just walks away leaving the Seller to engage the new Buyer in an agreement.
      - The Buyer might want to consider removing this provision because it seems to have the potential to cause problems.

- How can the Seller negotiate in good faith when he is out entertaining other offers?
- The escrow agent is not a part of the official Asset Purchase and Sale Agreement but is merely included in the main Agreement so as to give instructions to.
    - The escrow agent will thus sign the document on a separate signatory page.
- The letter of credit is good for $1,824,000.00 and partial drawing are permitted.
    - The letter of credit is signed by a bank officer.
- The bill of sale should be signed by both the Buyer and the Seller.
    - The Bill of sale is designed to convey ownership of an asset from one individual or entity to another.

APPENDIX 3 – REAL PROPERTY LEASE

- Title
  - The title is capitalized and centered and underlined.
    - This is generally considered proper from.
    - The title identifies the type of contract.
      - I would add "property" to the title so it reads "Property Lease" or add "real" and "property" so it reads "Real Property Lease."
- Definitions/Defined Terms
  - If it makes sense for some reason, definitions can be introduced "on the fly" in the first place they occur including in the preamble or introductory paragraph or the recitals.
  - All terms are nicely numbered and underlined making them stand out.
- This Real Property Lease is in a standard form and well written and organized.
- PREMISES
  - Good section and establishes the parameters for the lease.
- TERM
  - The term as an exact start date and end date which is clear and concise.
  - One sentence states that the Landlord is not liable nor shall the lease become void if the Landlord cannot deliver possession of the premises to the Tenant for reasons not created through negligence or fault.
    - This is bad for the Tenant because he might need immediate space and just because negligence or fault was not the reason behind the delay in delivering the premises does not due anything to help the Tenant and in fact causes injury to him.
    - The Tenant is left holding on to a lease that he cannot get out of and is at the same time ineffectual for his purposes.
    - The Tenant does not have to pay rent during this time but again the payment of rent is not the issue. The Tenant needs office space for which he has a lease for but cannot use.
    - Tenant must sue for ejectment.
    - Good example of risk shifting and allocation, whatever you think of the merits.

- Another sentence qualifies the previous mentioned sentence and states that if the Landlord cannot deliver possession of the premises to the Tenant by a certain date then the lease may be cancelled.
  - There is no need for the first sentence.
  - This sentence alone is enough to protect both interests.
  - The tenant would want to insert a particular date that is very close to the original commencement date; the landlord could argue for 30 days, i.e., enough time for a prompt ejectment/ eviction action.
- OPTION TO EXTEND TERM
  - What is a "period?"
    - Perhaps it is best to just state a certain amount of months or years.
  - This section sets the stage for how rent during the extended term will be calculated.
  - The Tenant must give the Landlord 60 days notice if he wants to extend.
    - What happens if the Tenant cannot give 60 days notice or only gives 30 days notice? Can the Tenant then no longer extend his lease? The lease as written does not say what happens.
- DETERMINATION OF RENT
  - The parties have 30 days after the landlord receives the Option Notice in which to agree on a monthly rent during the extended term.
    - Are these dates firm or can they be adjusted at the option of the Landlord?
    - If they can be adjusted, what is the rent if the 30 days extends into the Extended Term?
    - The lease does not address these concerns and does not make it clear if these dates are set in stone or if they have some flexibility to them.
  - The appointed real estate appraisers are not given much time to come up with a number.
    - The Landlord and the Tenant both have to find an appraiser and then those two appraisers have to agree on a third appraiser.
      - This can take a substantial amount of time.

- The appraisers then have to do their respective work and agree on a figure.
  - The lease states that if at least two of the three arbitrators appointed do not agree on a rental figure prior to the expiration of the Term, the reasonable rental rate shall be determined by computing the average.
    - This sentence is written in the negative.
      - It might read better if it says, "two of three arbitrators must agree on a number."
      - The average can be artificially high if the arbitrator selected by the Landlord inflates his estimate.
      - I would still want the option to back out of the lease if I do not like the number that the arbitrators come up with-in the formula of averages.
- If the appraisers fail for any reason to come up with a number then the rental rate shall be determined by a particular court.
  - This process that the Landlord and Tenant are contemplating will take much time. Much more time then I believe they are allowing themselves in the contract.
  - They have a very optimistic time frame for trying to come up with a new rental rate that is fair and acceptable to both parties.

- RENT
  - Rent addresses both the concern of real estate professionals and the average person who pays rent each month.

- o All installments of rent shall be paid at the office of the Landlord.
  - ▪ Does this mean hand delivered?
  - ▪ The contract does not speak to how it is to be paid.
  - ▪ Does lawful money include checks?
  - ▪ What if the Landlord and the Tenant have a falling out and the Landlord wants get rid of the Tenant.
    - • The lease allows the Landlord to designate a place for payment.
      - o The Landlord could require payment in person at a location across the country.
        - ▪ The possibility is unlikely but it can be contemplated.
        - ▪ It is necessary to think about the worst case scenarios and try to prepare a contract in anticipation of them.
  - ▪ There should be language that addresses the method of payment such as "US mail" and the word "reasonable" should be included to address the Landlord's ability to designate a location for payment.
- • ASSIGNMENT AND SUBLETTING
  - o There should be language that gives the Landlord the ability to deny any assignment or at least have the ability to check and verify potential assignment activity.
- • REPAIRS
  - o Is the Landlord responsible for light bulbs?
    - ▪ Maybe a list of certain things that the Landlord is responsible for could be helpful in this section.
  - o What is reasonable wear and tear?
    - ▪ Is reasonable defined by the circumstances of the business for which the lease space is being used and the Landlord has complete knowledge of?
      - • For instance:
        - o I rented a house in undergrad in Boulder Colorado with six other men and the landlord had us all on the lease so he had full knowledge that there were seven young men living in the house. A long story short – he

164

tried to sue for what he called "excessive wear and tear." Reasonable wear and tear is different depending on the usage. I would insert language that addresses things that I consider normal wear and tear.

- ALTERATIONS
  - As the Landlord I would want consent for any alterations that go on in my building. If nothing else, I would just like to know what is going on or planned to go on.
    - The value might increase with improvements but it might become harder to rent because the improvements are very specific to the tenant.
      - This presents a dilemma for the Landlord. The fair market value might increase but because of the specific improvements it could become much harder to rent. This is why as the Landlord I would want to know what actions the Tenant is taking in my building. Even good intentions and well intended actions can have negative consequences.
      - Does the Tenant have to stop remodeling if they are disrupting other tenant? The lease does not speak to what the remedy is for disrupting or disturbing other tenants.

- DESTRUCTION
  - The Tenant is in limbo for 45 days while the Landlord tries to figure out if he can get the building repaired within 120 days.
  - Is the Landlord responsible for restoring the premises to the way it looked before the Tenant took over possession or how it looked after the Tenant made substantial improvements to the space? The contract does not address this issue.
  - What is the remedy if the Tenant is told they will be able to move back in within 120 days but on day 119 the Landlord says it will be longer?

- SERVICES
  - The Landlord should be providing water and electricity not "reasonable" water and electricity? Does the Landlord plan

on charging for excessive bathroom use or excessive hand washing?

- o The Landlord only provides heat and air-conditioning during the hours of 8:00 to 6:00 daily except Saturdays, Sundays and public holidays and requires 24 hours notice to provide such services during these "other" hours and days.
  - I do not now what kind of business is being run out of the premises but I can foresee people working beyond 6 and having to do so without being able to provide 24 hours notice.
  - Maybe language should be incorporated to extend the hours or to always have such services available and just due away with the 24 hours requirement. The Landlord can still charge for such services but at least they will be available without notice having to be given.

- **INSURANCE**
  - o Is it customary to put a landlord on a tenant's insurance policy?
- **INSOLVENCY OR RECEIVERSHIP**
  - o The language should simply read as long as the Tenant continues to pay rent and is not delinquent on his payments the lease may not be terminated.
- **DEFAULT AND RE-ENTRY; RIGHT TO CURE**
  - o There should be language that requires the Landlord to take reasonable precautions in removing and/or storing the Tenant's belongings.
  - o The Landlord has the ability to re-let the premises even with the Tenants possessions still on the premises.
    - There should be language that requires the Landlord to remove any possessions, documents or computers and such before he can re-let the premises.
    - There should be specific language that says that the Landlord is required to mitigate his damages if the Tenant fails to pay rent or becomes delinquent in his rent payments. The lease addresses this concern but I would feel more comfortable if specific "mitigation of damages" language is actually used.
  - o What happens if the licensed real estate brokers cannot agree on the amount of rental loss that could have been reasonably avoided?

- REMOVAL OF PROPERTY
    - The Landlord may sell any and all such property at public or private sale after it has been stored for a period of 90 days.
        - This does not sound like a long period of time.
        - Is this legal? The Landlord does not need a court order to simply go and sell property that belongs to another person?
        - Does the Tenant have any method to challenge the price that the Landlord sold his possessions for or for that matter challenge the fact that the Landlord actually took ownership rights over his possessions and sold them? I would want language included that says something to the effect that if you, Landlord, sell my property you must get the fair market value for it and cannot accept any amount of money for such property that is below the fair market value. I would also want language that speaks to providing the Tenant with some kind of notice that his possessions are being sold.
- COST OF SUIT
    - This is a good clause and helps to prevent frivolous suits from being filed.
- TAX ON TENANT'S PROPERTY
    - The clause says that the Tenant has to pay the Landlord's taxes.
        - This does not sound fair.
        - The clause reads in the first part as saying that the Tenant is responsible for any taxes levied against Landlord or Landlord's property.
        - The clause then goes on to add "or" if the assessed value is increased by the inclusion of a value placed upon such personal property or trade fixtures of the Tenant. The clause does not say the Tenant is responsible for the difference in taxes assessed because of the inclusions. The clause simply says that the Tenant is responsible for taxes. I would like to see this language clarified because I do not see how the Tenant is responsible for taxes that are duly owed by the Landlord. **[of course, in a triple net lease, this is common]**
- RENTAL ADJUSTMENT

- Base Year should be defined immediately or referenced to where it is defined.
    - I thought that I had missed the definition of Base Year and began flipping back over the document while never thinking to flip forward.
    - The definition of Base Year should be readily apparent because it is the defining year for any rental adjustment.
- The word "practicable" should be replaced with "practical" for ease of reading and understanding.
- The Tenant should have the option to either pay the lump sum of additional rent due for the prior calendar year or have it prorated in the then current calendar year.
- **BASE YEAR**
    - Who is to decide what the "rentable" square footage is?
        - I would like to incorporate language that is similar to the Determination of Rent schedule.
    - It is good practice to protect the Tenant by inserting clause (d) into the lease agreement. This prevents the Landlord from excessive increases unless of course the percentage inserted is unfortunately high.
        - This percentage is an area of the lease in which a lawyer for the Tenant would want to fight hard for.
- **CONDEMNATION**
    - The Tenant has good language placed in the lease that speaks to his "opinion" of the premises as to whether or not it is suitable for his needs.
- **HOLDING OVER**
    - I would like to see language that says under no circumstances in the event of a holdover if rent is accepted should it be considered a month-to-month lease.
- **ENTRY AND INSPECTION**
    - There should be clear language that says the Landlord will not inconvenience the Tenant in any unreasonable way.
- **TIME**
    - What does this mean? It looks like a sentence from a novel not one that belongs in a property lease.
- **EXHIBIT A**
    - The last paragraph should be first before the list is presented to the Tenant regarding what the Landlord will furnish. If the Tenant has a hard number above which the Landlord will not pay the Tenant can then manipulate the

items listed so as to come as close as possible to the hard number without going over.

APPENDIX 4 - SETTLEMENT AGREEMENT

- SETTLEMENT AGREEMENT AND MUTUAL RELAEASE
  - The edits in the documents title and introduction tend to be more of form rather then substance.
    - The edits are designed to transform the document into plain English from the onset.
    - There is no need in either style or substance for the phrase "on the one hand/on the other hand."
    - The word "extinguish" is deleted because it tends to connote a negative image of the document and what the document is designed to accomplish.
    - The document is designed to "settle" the claims, disputes, and differences between the landlord and the tenant and the word "settle" tends to make it more appealing to the parties.
      - The document is not an adversarial one and the placement of the use of the word "settle" is much more appealing and appropriate.

- RECITALS
  - The recitals are intended to set the context for the agreement and are useful in later interpretations.
  - The recitals should as well be written in plain English.
  - Recitals are designed to let the reader the grasp the nature, purpose, and basis of the agreement.
    - The use of the "whereas" does not need to be included because it is not commonly used in the English language and can be confusing and is redundant throughout the document.
    - The use of letters to separate the facts of the recital are useful for organization and ease of reading.
    - The edits make it easy to simply grasp the facts and the reason is clearly understood why the document is being formed.
    - The edits in the recital allows for easy and clear reading.
- AGREEMENT
  - The use of the phrase "now , therefore" is not plain English.
  - The deletion of the statement about terms, provisions, conditions, agreement, payment, releases, warranties, and representations is necessary because it does not belong.

- It appears that this is just a form agreement and the drafter did not take the time to exclude the provisions that are not applicable.
- The use of underlining allows the reader to clearly see the main obligations of the agreement. The tenant has to vacate the premises and pay a certain amount of money.
- The drafter separates out the tenants payment obligations which is clear and concise. It is much easier to read a payment obligation or schedule that is not in a paragraph form.
- The document uses the active voice by clearly stating what the tenant has to do. The tenant "shall execute" and the documents deletes other phrases that give the tenant the ability to confer his obligations onto another person.
- The use of the word "said" is not necessary and does not add anything to the document and is not plain English.
- By not labeling the exhibits in this section the drafter can attach any documents that he feels are relevant at the end.
  - By simply stating "copies are attached as exhibits" gives the drafter flexibility in what he chooses to include as exhibits and allows final editing to be easier.
- DEFAULT
  - It is easier to just use the word "tenant" instead of writing in the persons name before the use of the word "tenant" after it has been clearly understood who the tenant is as defined in the opening.
  - It is more clear to just say "if tenant fails to make any payment" instead of "fails to make one or more" which can be ambiguous.
  - It is much easier to just say that the landlord can notify the tenant of default by mail instead of getting in to the legality of what the landlord will then be entitled to.
  - The use of the word "only" in reference to how a default is cured is important because it is clear and to the point and leaves no room for misinterpretations about how the default can be cured.
  - The drafter included language here about his remedies should a default occur and it is clear and concise.
- MUTUAL RELEASE
  - *No edits
- LATER DISCOVERED FACTS
  - The use of the word "hereafter" again is unnecessary and is not plain English.
  - The drafter added language that makes it clear that they are talking about future facts.
  - The drafter deleted unnecessary language perhaps so not to limit

what future facts might be considered. The drafter simply stated "with respect to the claims" in anticipation of facts that possibly can arise which are not listed or contemplated at the time of the original draft.

- WAIVER OF CIVIL CODE SECTION 1542
  - Language is deleted that is not plain English and redundant.
- FUNDAMNEATL FAIRNESS
  - Representations and Warranties is deleted because it does not belong here and the use of the phrase "fundamental fairness" is more appropriate.
  - This section is written in plain English and well reasoned and easy to understand. It is designed to explain to the tenant that any ambiguities that he might have before signing the document should be resolved because the applicable drafting laws as they pertain to ambiguities will not apply. (can you draft around applicable state or federal laws?)
  - The obligations of the tenant are put in paragraph form as opposed to breaking them down into lettered sections.
    - I am not sure why it is put into paragraph form but maybe one explanation is that it looks as if the tenant would have to sign after each statement on the original draft or initial each statement indicating that he read them and understands them.
    - I find it easier to read when items are broken down into lists but the paragraph form on the edited version is clear and perhaps the edit was done for formatting reasons and/or space.
- NO PRIOR ASSIGNMENT
  - There is no need for the use of the word "covenants" in this section and "no prior agreement" is easy to understand what this section is dealing with.
    - Again by simply stating "claim" the drafter is not limiting himself to a list that could be ambiguous or considered exhaustive.
    - Heretofore is not plain English and does not belong.
    - The original draft section is long and cumbersome and uses words that are not plain English.
      - The edited version breaks down what was long and not well written and hard to understand into a paragraph that is short, concise and to the point.
- ATTORNEY FEES
  - The edited version used the active voice and says "shall" recover

all attorney's fees involved and says "shall" not be limited to reasonable attorney fees.
- The edited version does not get into what fees will be covered and what fees will not be covered and the drafter does not limit himself or the fees that might be applicable.
- AGREEMENT BINDING ON SUCCESSORS
  - Only language edits are incorporated in order to keep the consistency of the document in plain English.
- GOVERNING LAW
  - *No edits
- SEVERABILITY
  - The drafter again does not include a list of terms that could be considered as exhaustive. Instead the drafter uses language that is broad so as not to tie his hands in possible future litigation.
  - The drafter changed the language around in an effort to make it more clear but the substance did not change.
- COUNTERPARTS
  - *No edits
- ENTIRE AGREEMENT
  - The drafter broke down the main points of this section into letters which make it easy to read and follow but the substance did not change.
  - The drafter again deleted language that is not plain English.
  - The drafter again uses broad language where he can and tries to limit the use of lists.
  - The drafter incorporates the use of the phrase "statement or promise" in sections a, b, and c in order to clearly define what he considers as the entire agreement.
  - NO IMPLIED WAIVER
    - There are edit marks but the only edit that is really incorporated into the final draft is the deletion of the phrase "or more times" and "or times" and this is simply done to eliminate unnecessary language
  - CONSTRUCTUION
    - This section is deleted because it is unnecessary and covered earlier and thus redundant.

- Old English language is deleted and the revised draft simply states "AGREED" and that is all that is necessary with a slight change in the signing and dating areas.

APPENDIX 5 - VENDOR ORIENTAL SOFTWARE
LISCENSE AGREEMENT

A sample student analysis is below.

Overview

It appears from an initial reading of this agreement that it was prepared by the Company with probably little negotiations with the Customer or input from them. It appears to be a contract drafted by the Company and presented to the Customer as "take it or leave it." Because the agreement is for the use of software the Company is in a much more advantageous bargaining position then the customer. Perhaps the Company is the only organization that makes the particular software that the Customer needs. If this is the case, the Company can certainly define the parameters of the agreement without much thought to negotiations with the Customer. The extensive use of the word "shall" in reference to the Customer in the first three pages of the agreement alone indicates that this agreement is primarily designed to protect the interests of the Company and only offered to the Customer for their signature.

- The title is not underlined.
- There is no introductory paragraph.
  - The first paragraph of the agreement could identify the parties and the type of transaction that they are documenting
  - The introductory paragraph should be written out more in a paragraph form as opposed to the form used on the Vendor Oriented Agreement. The Vendor Oriented Agreement does establish defined terms for the parties and provides a reference date for the document but the introductory paragraph could be more of a 'paragraph.'
- There are no recitals.
  - It is difficult to grasp the nature, purpose, and basis of the agreement from the onset because there are no background facts given.
  - An appropriate recital will include the following:
    - The relationship and goals of the parties.
    - The nature of the transaction.
    - Other transactional documents.
  - A provision regarding the accuracy of the recitals should be expressed clearly in the main agreement.

- There should be an easy transition from the recitals to the substantive portion of the agreement.
    - In order to enhance the reading of the document the defined terms section should be located near the beginning of the agreement.
- There should be a table of contents.
    - Even though the Vendor Oriented Agreement divides the sections of the agreement up rather well, a table of contents would allow a reader to quickly locate those sections more easily.
- There should be a well defined information schedule.
    - The contract extends to the customer and its affiliates for use during the ordinary course of business. Affiliates should be identified by name in the form of a list.

- INSTALLATION AND TRAINING
    - It might be helpful in this section to specify the designated locations for installation of the software and to try and define or limit the number of people who will receive training from the Company.
- COMPANY'S OTHER OBLIGATGIONS
    - All support services for Customer are provided by phone except when Customer and Company agree that on-site services are necessary to diagnose or resolve the failure.
        - It is foreseeable that the Company and the Customer will not always agree when on-site services are necessary and there is not a triggering event for this service to be rendered.
        - The contract should say something to the effect that when the Company cannot resolve the problem after two attempts over the phone, on-site service shall be performed.
    - Is the Customer only eligible for upgrades that are provided to the Company's general customer base or is the Customer entitled to all Company upgrades? The contract affirmatively says both.
        - Perhaps an upgrade will present itself that only is beneficial to the Customer. According to one sentence in the contract the Customer would be eligible for this upgrade free of charge.
        - However, another sentence says the Customer is only eligible for upgrades at no additional cost

when those upgrades are available to the Company's general customer base.

- The contract should affirmatively state what the Customer is entitled to in order to prevent confusion on the part of the Customer and the Company.

o The Company has the sole discretion to determine when updates are necessary and the Company has to promptly install such upgrades.

- What if the upgrades change the function of the program in a substantial way? Will the Company have to retrain the employees of the Customer. What if the Customer is not satisfied with a certain aspect of the software? According to the contract the Customer does not have any influence over the Company in releasing an upgrade. What if the Customer does not want the upgrade? According to the contract the Customer has to install all upgrades.

- Perhaps the contract should speak to the dilemma of when an upgrade does not benefit the Customer but rather is detrimental to them and their business.

o Professional Services

- Is the list of professional services inclusive?
- Is the Company's standard professional rate the same for all the professional services listed?
- The Company reserves the right to charge a premium for services outside the normal business hours but this premium is never defined in terms of a number, percent, or industry norms.

- CUSTOMER'S OTHER OBLIGATINS

o What does it mean for the Customer to be responsible to provide all other resources 'reasonably necessary' to install the software and to begin using it?

- Perhaps a list would be helpful here to define or provide an example of what other resources the contract is contemplating.

o Data Security

- An example or a reference to an example that identifies what the Customer needs to do in order to adequately protect the confidentiality and intellectual property rights of the Company would be helpful.

- PAYMENTS
  - Support Fees Payment
    - Continuing for thirty (30) months the Customer shall pay to the Company quarterly support fees. This length of time strikes me as long as an initial period.
    - Instead of ongoing support services automatically renewing for one additional (30) thirty month period unless the Customer gives notice to terminate on-going support services, the contract should simply state that after thirty (30) months the contract term will terminate.
      - The Customer could be given the option to renew not the option to decline automatic renewal.
    - On any annual basis the Company may increase support fees.
      - A possible increase of 10% is significant per year.
      - Can the Company raise fees every year?
        - A possible cap on the percentage increase in service fees throughout the life of the contract could serve to protect the Customer from excessive price increases.
  - Expense Reimbursement
    - Customer shall reimburse Company for its reasonable travel, lodging, meals, and related expense.
      - Is this list inclusive?
      - What is reasonable travel?
        - Private Jet
        - First Class
        - Coach
        - Luxury car rentals
        - Public transportation
        - Budget motels
        - Five star resorts
        - Gas reimbursement
      - What is related expense?
        - Entertainment
        - Unforeseen expenses

- Food
- Taxes
  - Customer shall promptly reimburse Company for any taxes payable or collected by the Company.
    - 'Promptly' should be specified with a number such as "within thirty days of receipt".
    - Promptly to one person can mean a much different thing to another person.
- Payment Terms
  - It is interesting that the interest rate is set at 12% per annum (or if lower, the maximum rate permitted by law). This shows how little influence the Customer had in drafting this contract.

VI. Sample Additional Exercises

ASSIGNMENT #1

Your client, David Taylor, has recently created a corporation for the purpose of purchasing and operating a Hallmark Card Shop. The name of the corporation is Taylor Enterprises, Inc., with Mr. Taylor being the sole shareholder.

Mr. Taylor's grandfather, Richard Franklin, has agreed to help his grandson in the purchase of the store by providing a capital loan to the corporation in the amount of $100,000. However, Mr. Franklin is insistent that the matter be handled at arm's length, with all the proper documentation, etc.

The parties have agreed that the principal shall be repaid in five equal annual installments of $20,000, payable on or before December 31 of each calendar year, with the first payment being due December 31, 20__. Throughout the term of the loan, interest shall be payable monthly, with payments due on the 1st and delinquent on the 10th. Interest payments shall commence October 1, 2001, and will continue each and every month for so long as there is any principal balance outstanding. The interest rate applicable for 200_ shall be 8-1/2%. Beginning January 1, 20__, and for each year thereafter, the interest rate will be adjusted annually (either up or down) to a rate equal to the prime rate as reported in the Money Rates section of the *Wall Street Journal* as of the first day of publication for each succeeding year.

Mr. Franklin wants a waiver of notice or demand, an acceleration clause in the event of default, and a standard attorney's fee provision. He also wants a waiver of presentment, protest, and notice of nonpayment. As a concession to his grandson, Mr. Franklin is willing to make the loan unsecured. However, he does want David Taylor as a co-obligor on the note.

Your assignment is to prepare a promissory note for Mr. Taylor complying with the terms as outlined above.

ASSIGNMENT #2

Your client, Jenney Spenser, has reached a tentative agreement to purchase the Franklin Inn, a bed and breakfast inn located at 123 Franklin Road, Rugby, Tennessee. The inn is currently owned jointly by Debbie and Michael Smith, a married couple. The tentative terms of the agreement are as follows:

Ms. Spenser will purchase the inn, which consists of a two-story, five thousand square-foot Victorian-style dwelling located on three acres of property. None of the current contents of the building will be sold.

The parties would like to close within the next ninety days.

The Smiths are willing to warrant clear title and will give an environmental warranty. However, given the age of the dwelling (twenty-three years) they are not willing to warrant the physical condition of the property. Accordingly, Ms. Spenser wants a sixty-day period in which to bring an engineer onto the premises for the purpose of inspecting its physical condition. If Ms. Spenser is not satisfied with the condition of the building, she wants the ability to back out of the contract.

Ms. Spenser has put together a business plan for the operation of the bed and breakfast inn and has budgeted a fixed amount of money for debt service. It is essential that she be able to obtain ninety percent financing for the purchase for a 30-year loan at a rate of interest not in excess of eight percent. If he is unable to secure this financing, he needs to be able to get out of the contract.

Ms. Spenser will pay $5,000 down upon execution of the contract, with the balance to be paid at closing.

Ms. Spenser would like you to prepare a draft agreement to present to Mr. and Mrs. Smith. They currently do not have a lawyer, but they will probably get someone to review the agreement before they sign it. Ms. Spenser understands that there may be other items which need to be included in the contract, and she is relying upon you to advise her accordingly.

Your assignment is to prepare a summary outline of the agreement that contains the numbered paragraphs, paragraph headings, and a very brief summary of what each paragraph would contain using appropriate terminology to identify the sorts of provisions to be used. The purpose of this exercise is for you to identify the various issues that need to be addressed in the agreement. You are not required to actually draft the agreement.

ASSIGNMENT #3

Your client, Joseph Hunter, is contemplating marriage in the near future to Jennifer Morgan. Mr. Hunter would like for you to prepare a prenuptial agreement for them.

Mr. Hunter is fifty-seven years old and is the seventy percent owner of Hunter Enterprises, Inc., a family owned business. Mr. Hunter recently had the business appraised at a value of approximately $3.2 million. Mr. Hunter's first and only wife passed away about six years ago. He has three adult sons, each of whom are active in the family business. The balance of Mr. Hunter's assets consists of his home in Knoxville, Tennessee, a condominium in Charleston, South Carolina, a retirement account valued at approximately $800,000, and various other investments, personal property, etc. His total net worth is approximately $3.5 million.

Ms. Morgan is forty-two years old. Her first marriage ended in divorce approximately five years ago. Ms. Morgan is a law professor at the University of Tennessee in Knoxville. She is self sufficient, has a comfortable income, and has net assets of approximately $250,000.

Mr. Hunter cares very deeply for Ms. Morgan, and feels very positive that their marriage will be a good one. Nevertheless, he is also aware of the fact that he has amassed, through many years of hard work, a significant amount of wealth, the bulk of which he intends to pass to his three sons. If he were to die, he intends to make generous provisions for Ms. Morgan in his will. However, he does not want her to acquire a vested interest in his property simply by reason of their marriage and does not want to risk his estate in a divorce if the marriage does not work out.

In Mr. Hunter's opinion, all property that the parties bring to the marriage should remain their own separate property to dispose of however they see fit. Any property acquired after marriage should be deemed to be owned as it is titled when acquired.

Your assignment is to prepare a prenuptial agreement under which the parties waive all marital rights in each others' separate premarital assets in the event of either death or divorce. Furthermore, in the event the parties divorce, there should be no support obligations from one party to another. Assets acquired subsequent to marriage should be disposed of as per Mr. Hunter's instructions.

ASSIGNMENT #4

You represent Fortner Development, LLC, a limited liability company that is engaged in real estate development. The company is in the process of completing construction on Fortner Plaza Mall, a retail shopping mall, located in San Diego, California, adjacent to the site of a new major league baseball complex.

The mall owner and developer, Donna Fortner, has asked that you prepare standard commercial leases for the retail tenants in the new mall.

For purposes of this assignment, you do not need to draft the entire lease. Rather, please draft those provisions dealing with a tenant's default and the landlord's remedies.

Ms. Fortner's only direction with regard to default/remedies is that she wants a very tough agreement that will afford her the greatest latitude allowed by law in dealing with a troublesome tenant. Because of minor cost overruns in construction, the operating capital for the shopping mall will be somewhat marginal for the first several years of operation. Accordingly, she must be able to deal quickly and decisively with tenants who are late or delinquent in their payments.

ASSIGNMENT #5

You have been retained by Ms. Young and Ms. Pierce to represent them in the formation of a new corporation. The corporation will produce a weekly television show during which the two principals will offer their thoughts and reviews concerning recently released movies and videos.

Ms. Young and Ms. Pierce are sophisticated businesspersons and understand the necessity of having a shareholders agreement. One item that they want to specifically address is that of conflict resolution. While they have been in business together for some time, they acknowledge the fact that differences could arise between them that would make their remaining in business together impractical.

Accordingly, as part of the shareholders agreement that you will prepare for them, they want to include a cross purchase provision. The provision should allow for either of them to make an offer to purchase the other's interest, which offer will also constitute an offer to sell.

Your assignment is to draft a cross purchase provision for inclusion in the shareholders agreement. For purpose of this exercise only, you may not use a form book or any other outside form. You should draft this provision yourself.

In your cross-sell provision, you should cover the mechanics of making the initial offer, the time period and mechanics by which the offeree shareholder must decide to purchase or sell, and the mechanics for closing.

ASSIGNMENT #6

You represent Carmen Breslauer, a retired engineer who now dabbles in the real estate market. Ms. Breslauer has recently purchased a number of homes in the University area, which she has renovated, and is leasing to graduate students.

You have been given Ms. Breslauer's basic lease agreement that she uses for each of her properties. Typically, she leases each home for a one-year term. However, a proposed tenant, with good references, has recently asked if she would add a renewal option to the lease for an additional one year term. Given the cost of advertising for new tenants, Ms. Breslauer is happy to oblige under the following conditions.

If Ms. Breslauer has had any problems with the tenant during the initial term of the lease, she doesn't want the tenant to be able to renew. Furthermore, if the tenant does renew, rent during the second one year term should be increased by ten percent (10%). Obviously, if the tenant elects to renew, Ms. Breslauer will need some sort of ample notice provision so that she will know whether or not she needs to advertise the property. Ms. Breslauer also suggests you feel free to put anything in the renewal provision you think she needs.

Your assignment is to draft a renewal option provision for inclusion in the standard lease agreement.

ASSIGNMENT #7

Your client, Dr. William Coombe, has recently left his position as the Chief Attending Physician of San Diego's Scripps/La Jolla Hospital to open a general family medical practice in Knoxville. (He wanted a calmer, less crowded environment.) Dr. Coombe has decided to hire a second physician who will specialize in children and pediatric matters. He has interviewed his good friend Doug Ross and wants to offer him an employment contract. However, while Doug is an excellent doctor, Bill is aware that Doug's behavior can be "erratic" at times and accordingly, Bill wants a fair amount of latitude in terminating the contract if necessary.

Generally speaking, Bill wants to be able to terminate the contract at any point in time if Doug does anything "wrong," but he doesn't know exactly what that might include.

He also wants to be able to terminate the contract for no reason at all if he chooses to but is willing to pay Doug three months severance pay should he do so.

If Doug should decide to leave, that's ok, but he wants Doug to give him at least one month notice before leaving.

Assuming that a general employment agreement has already been prepared, your assignment is to draft a paragraph dealing with termination of the agreement that incorporates and addresses Dr. Coombe's proposals. You may use form books for this assignment.

ASSIGNMENT # 8

Community Church operates various ministries for the lower income members of the local community. For many years, the Church has operated a community food bank where donated goods and packaged food products are distributed to the needy on a regular basis. The church has also recently begun operating a free automotive clinic one Saturday a month at the church, where the poor, elderly, etc., can have their oil and filters changed, antifreeze checked, windshield wipers replaced, and tires rotated. The clinic doesn't do any repair work per se. Both the food bank and automotive clinic are staffed by members of the church who volunteer their time.

The pastor of the church feels that these programs are important and is pleased to be able to offer these services to the community. However, he is also aware of how litigious society has become and recently heard of a church being sued over a similar activity.

The pastor has asked if you would donate your legal services by drafting releases for both the food bank and the automotive clinic. He doesn't know what needs to be said but would like to know that the church and volunteer workers are protected.

Your assignment is to prepare a release either for the food bank or the automotive clinic.

ASSIGNMENT # 9

You represent Acme Food Products, Inc., a Delaware corporation that produces and distributes various lines of food products throughout the Eastern United States. Acme has recently negotiated the purchase of all of the stock of Woodsmoke Beef Jerky, Inc., a small corporation located in Atlanta, Georgia, which produces and sells various lines of beef jerky to local food retailers, convenience stores, etc. Woodsmoke is owned by Carmel and Christy Littleton, who started the business about seven years ago as a cottage industry. The business has grown significantly, having gross sales in 1999 of $3.5 million. The Littletons, who own all of the stock of the corporation, are active in the business, along with their sons and daughter.

In conjunction with the purchase of the business, Acme desires to enter into non-compete agreements with the appropriate parties. They have asked that you prepare a draft non-compete agreement that will restrict the Littletons from engaging in competitive activities for a period of seven years.

ASSIGNMENT #10

You have been asked by James Kirk to represent him in structuring and documenting the purchase of a new business. Mr. Kirk has negotiated the purchase of a hobby shop located in Daly City, California, that specializes in model rockets, spacecraft, and other associated paraphernalia.

For $750,000.00, Mr. Kirk is purchasing the land and building where the store is located, along with all assets, inventory, equipment, furniture, fixtures, and other associated personal property. Intending to devote more time to his medical practice, the seller, Leonard McCoy, has agreed not to open another hobby shop within San Francisco or San Mateo Counties, for the next 5 years.

The purchase price will be paid by delivery of $100,000.00 down at closing, with the balance to be financed by Dr. McCoy over a five-year period. Mr. Kirk will grant Dr. McCoy a lien on all assets purchased to secure the financing.

Mr. Kirk plans to incorporate the business under the name of Trek Enterprises, LLC. This limited liability company will be formed before the purchase and will be identified as the buyer in all necessary documents.

Briefly list each legal document that will be required in order to complete the transaction as noted above and outline the principle provisions for each document that you identify.

ASSIGNMENT #11

Drafting a partnership Agreement[19]

Name and Occupation

You are Ted McAllester, and you are a real estate developer, living in Knoxville. You have developed primarily commercial real estate projects in the East Tennessee area.

New Business Venture

You have been involved in discussions with Dana Hearn, an Olympic silver medalist in the kayak single slalom event in the 1996 Olympics. The two of you have decided to open an outdoor outfitting shop on the Ocoee River, with you supplying the financial backing and retail knowledge and Hearn supplying the outdoor outfitting knowledge and reputation. You have tentatively decided on the name of "Appalachian outfitters."

Partner

Your partner, Dana Hearn, has just won the silver medal in the 1996 Olympic single slalom kayak event. He is about 28 years old, and has been well-known in the canoe and kayak sporting world for several years. He has been a representative for Dagger Canoe Co. canoes, kayaks and water sport equipment, and has received endorsements for Patagonia water sport clothing.

Building/Ocoee River Location

You have purchased a S-acre tract on the Ocoee River for $225.000. The property is improved with an old buildin9 which will need to be expanded and renovated. The estimated cost of renovations will be $175,000. After renovations, the building will have about 2,500 square feet. You are contemplating keeping the real property in your name and leasing it to the partnership.

---

19 Thank you to Adjunct Professor Brian Krumm of Knoxville Tennessee, used by permission.

Partnership Percentages

You propose that the partnership interests should be:

66 2/3 --yours
33 1/3 --Hearn

You have based this calculation on the estimated, original capital contributions. You will be investing about $120.000 for start-up inventory and equipment. Hearn is investing about $60,000 of his own money from endorsements, but he is asking that greater credit be given for name-recognition and expertise.

You are not opposed to allowing Hearn to buy a greater percentage in the partnership by buying out a portion of your capital contribution. You wish to keep at least a 50% ownership interest, however.

Capital contributions/Funding

You estimate initial start-up costs for inventory and equipment (cash register, computers, shelving and other supplies) to be about $180,000.

Operating Expenses

You have estimated the monthly operating costs of the business to be about $7,000.00, including costs for utilities, insurance, advertising, property taxes, salaries for part-time clerks and Hearn, withholding taxes, accounting services, and any new lines of inventory added.

Profits from Operations

Generally, profits payable to the partners will be declared after the operating expenses have been paid. The costs of replacing the inventory sold have been used to buy new inventory, and a reserve fund of 5% of total profits has been set aside for emergencies, equipment replacement or other undetermined, future needs.

If the Business Does Not Generate a Profit

During the months that the business does not generate a profit, the business will draw upon the reserve fund. Until a reserve is established, the partners will agree to make additional capital contributions commensurate with their partnership interests.

Accounts and Bookkeeping

An accountant will handle the bookkeeping and filing of taxes.

Daily Management of Business

Hearn will be handling day-to-day on-site operation of the business if because of his expertise in the outdoor outfitting area. Business decisions, such as new inventory lines and major expenditures must be decided by both partners. However, the daily work will be managed by Hearn.

Hearn to work in Business; salary

You have decided that Hearn may draw a base salary of $1,000.00 per month for operating the business on a daily full-time basis. In addition to his salary, he will draw his 33 1/3 percentage of the profits. You do not want to pay Hearn any more in salary because you want to keep him motivated to promote the business to obtain higher profits for the partnership.

In exchange for the salary, Hearn will agree to devote his full-time to the business, with the exception of continuing to compete in kayaking events and endorsements of certain products. You believe, however, that these outside activities should never take place during the week-day operating hours of 10:00 a.m. until 5:00 p.m.

Partnership Meetings

The two partners will speak frequently in person or by phone. The partnership should meet at least once monthly.

Future of Business/potential Rafting & Canoeing Business

You and Hearn intend to expand the business sometime in the future into leading rafting and canoeing trips on the Ocoee River. You want to wait to see how this outdoor shop works out, how profitable it is, and how you and your new partner work together before beginning this phase of the business.

The business may need to incorporate at that point or become a limited liability company, in order to handle the potential liability.

Dissolution of Partnership

The partnership will be automatically dissolved under the following conditions:

(a)   Death of either partner. You would want the opportunity to buy out the other partner's share, and Hearn will probably want the same right.

(b)   Bankruptcy of either partner.

(c)   Choice of either partner. Both partners want the right to buyout the interest of the other, with the value of the partnership interests to be valued by "the "accountant.

CONTRACT DRAFTING[20]

Harold Harrison is the owner of Bailey's Health Club located in West Knoxville. Harold has decided that he is ready to retire, and wishes to sell the Club.

Bailey's Health Club consists of a building of approximately 25,000 square feet, located on approximately 20 acres of real property at 1234 Papermill Drive. The Club is fully equipped with sports and exercise equipment, some of which is getting a little dated and will soon need to be replaced. A new Olympic size pool was put in about two years ago, and the indoor racquetball and tennis courts were recently refurbished. The outdoor tennis and basketball facilities are useable but in disrepair. The Club currently has 3,212 members but membership fluctuates between approximately 2,800 and 3,400 members. Dues range from $600 per year for certain limited memberships up to a package of $1200 per year which includes personal training sessions and group exercise classes. The Club has provided a steady income for Harold over the twelve years that he has owned and operated the Club. He employs about a dozen employees to run the club and sell memberships, and has special arrangements with about 15 instructors for such activities as tennis, racquetball yoga, aerobics, etc.. In addition he has special arrangements with personal trainers who are paid directly by the members but who must be approved by Bailey's.

Harold has entered into discussions with Barbara Muhlbeier and Clifford Cruze, two individuals who have agreed to go into business together (Cruzbeier Enterprises) for the purchase of Bailey's Club and properties. Harold is asking $12 million for the sale of the properties and Club, however, he is willing to sell the Club itself and not the properties. If Cruzbeier Enterprises elects to purchase the club only, then Harold will agree to enter into a lease with the terms to be negotiated.

The firm of Chase, Dothard, Henley, & Thurber will represent Harold Harrison.

---

20 Thank you to adjunct professor Brian Krumm of Knoxville Tennessee. Used by permission.

The firm of Barca, Buttry, Googe, and Moses will represent Ms. Muhlbeier and Mr. Cruze

The Firms will meet with their respective clients on April 6, 2003 to ask all relevant questions concerning their clients' proposals, plans, and circumstances. The Chase Firm will ultimately be responsible for drafting an Asset Sales Agreement for the parties. The Barca Firm will be responsible for drafting the Lease Agreement.

Assignments: **The Assignments are due on the dates outlined on the Syllabus**.

The only way you can contact your client concerning any questions about the deal must be made via. Anticipate a reply within 1 business day.

I would like each of you to keep track of the hours you spent on this assignment for billing purposes. Also, I would like each of you to anonymously rate your partners, on a scale of 3.0 - 4.0, in tenths of their contribution, both intellectually and functionally, to the accomplishment of the final products.

HIGHSCHOOLTOCOLLEGE.COM

HYPOTHETICAL FACTS AND INFORMATION[21]

This is a hypothetical fact pattern. Any similarity to any company, person, enterprise or thing whatsoever is wholly coincidental. Although based in part on a collection of actual events, all names have been changed.

These materials are the basic information you will need for this simulation and its negotiation and documentation. They may be supplemented with additional, party-specific information as the exercise proceeds.

---

[21] Note that all dates should be adjusted to bring these facts "forward" to the current period in which the assignment is given.

Business Description:

HighSchooltoCollege.Com (the "Company") was founded by Paul and Mary Hamstead, two technology savvy business school graduates that developed a business model while in their second year of business school, which Mary attended after dropping out of her second year of law school because of the workload. It is essentially a marketing conduit aimed at high school and college students in the United States.

The Company derives revenue primarily through the sale of sponsorships, advertising and other promotional services. It also generates fees from its various commercial relationships. To date, the Company has registered over 5.6 million members, and during December 2002 its web site generated approximately 500 million page views according to third party monitors. During the same period, WebWorld Magazine awarded the company's web site with its coveted "Da Bomb" award.

The Company has established a central hub that acts as an intermediary between students and key elements of the High School and College experience, including proprietary technology that allows members to instantly identify and contact other members based on specific criteria, such as school, major, location, place of birth, hobbies and interests. The Company provides its members with instant messengering, universal integrated e-mail and voicemail services, which can be accessed through the internet or telephonically. The Company also provides its members with other communication and posting services that allows members to share experiences and communicate among themselves.

Since its inception, the Company has not generated enough revenue to cover the substantial amounts it has spent to create, launch and enhance its products and services. In calendar year 2001, the Company generated revenues of $2.9 million, incurred operating expenses of $23 million, and took charges on its balance sheet of an additional $5.6 million of non-cash charges, such as depreciation, amortization and stock-based compensation. This resulted in a net loss of $25.7 million. Calendar year 2002 was better for the Company, but it still failed to show a profit: Revenues climbed to $10 million, operating expenses dropped to $20 million, and non-cash charges dropped to $4 million, leaving a net loss of $14 million.

Despite these financial results, the Company believes that its business model is solid and that it is well positioned to succeed over the long term in the evolving new economy. In the U.S. alone there are over 25 million students attending high schools and colleges or universities. Increasingly, students are using the internet to enhance the school experience, simplify the academic process and buy and sell goods and services. Market watchers estimate that student total spending power was over $200 billion in 2001, and that high school and college students made online purchases totaling over $800 million during the same period. Online purchases by this same group are expected to grow to between $2.5 and $3 billion by 2005. From a marketing perspective, high school and college students have been a difficult demographic to reach due to their active and mobile lifestyles and unpredictable consumption of conventional media. The Company believes that the internet and its unique portal and membership base is an effective mechanism for accessing these students.

The Company had projected that it would "go public" through an IPO in late 2000 or early 2001. However, as the IPO market for technology companies had softened, the Company began to look for a strategic partner or buyer that would infuse more cash and the potential for further growth into the Company through an acquisition of the Company or substantially all of its assets. After a few failed courtships, the Company has decided that it would like to pursue negotiations with TakeAdvantageOfStudents, Inc. a multi-national concern based in Newport, Rhode Island.

TakeAdvantagOfStudents, Inc. is in the business of providing internet "clearing house" and "ombudsman" services that relate to the worldwide student market. It is a public company, and its stock price has been very volatile, ranging from $35 at the beginning of 2000 to $4 presently – in the last weeks its trading range has been between $7 and $3, with no clear rhyme or reason. Earnings per share were -$0.56 for calendar year 2000, -$0.40 for calendar year 2001, and -$0.04 in 2002 – hopefully leading to positive profits in 2003.

TakeAdvantageOfStudents links providers of goods and services to students with those students – providing them with one stop access to a variety of discount coupons and promotional offers from companies such as Proctor & Gample, AHAP, Harcourt, Brace, Volonovich and the like, as well as student loan providers, loan consolidators, credit card companies and magazine publishers. These companies pay TakeAdvantageOfStudents a flat fee for the initial link, and 0.4% of the gross amount of any transactions that are obtained as a result of a link. In an effort to curtail excessive attorneys' fees, and to further pander to the student audience, the Company, TakeAdvantageOfStudents, Inc., and Paul and Mary have decided to let this class serve as their counsel. Groups of students will represent the buyer, seller and the insiders of the sellers over a structured negotiation and documentation of the deal. Counsel to buyers, sellers and insiders will meet to discuss strategy and progress, will seek guidance from their clients on business decisions, and will then conduct negotiations with opposing counsel.

Balance Sheet

As of December 31, 2002

ASSETS $17,525,019.83

Real Property $0.00
Personal Property..$17,525,019.83
Petty Cash $2,054.64
Depository Accts..$743,627.00
Security Deposits $239,269.97
Stock of Subsidiaries $309,128.11
Accounts Receivable...$3,687,389.49
Loan Payable (Pres.) $100,000.00
Intellectual Property...$5,000,000.00
Rolling Stock $75,000.00
Office Eq./Supplies...$41,530.00
Machinery..$2,504,025.00
Goodwill $5,000,000.00

LIABILITIES AND STOCKHOLDERS EQUITY $17,525,019.83

LIABILITIES[22] $12,345,048.61
Secured Debt..$0.00
Accrued Wages & Taxes $361,288.79
General Unsecured Debt..$11,983,759.82

STOCKHOLDER'S EQUITY $5,179,971.22

---

[22] Note that the listing of liabilities is not in GAAP format – it is in the form of distinctions that are largely relevant to legal, as opposed to business or accounting, analysis of the debt structure of the company.

Officers:

Paul Hamstead
HighSchooltoCollege.Com
4231 South Beach Drive
Miami, Florida

Mary Ortiz
HighSchooltoCollege.Com
4231 South Beach Drive
Miami, Florida

Sole Director:

Paul Hamstead
HighSchooltoCollege.Com
4231 South Beach Drive
Miami, Florida

State of Incorporation: Delaware

Paul is 29, Mary is 31. Note that Paul and Mary were formerly married
but separated two years ago, their divorce was final as of 3/30/00. Neither
has remarried. The divorce was fairly amicable, but some tensions
remain. They have no children.

Shareholders:

Paul Hamstead   1,000,000 shares common stock
HighSchooltoCollege.Com
4231 South Beach Drive
Miami, Florida

Mary Ortiz   1,000,000 shares common stock
HighSchooltoCollege.Com
4231 South Beach Drive
Miami, Florida

Various Venture Capitalists,   5,000,000 shares
PreferredMedia Partners and Friends
Class A Stock, Featuring 6% of Paul & Mary Cumulative Dividend,
Convertible To Common Stock upon Public Offering; Liquidation
Preference

Many of the entities with which the Company has contracted with for content and linked services are equity holders. These parties have already received their shares of stock, generally under agreements that are separate from (and often not even referenced in) the contracts that govern the on-going relationships. These entities are likely to be very disappointed if the sale does not produce enough funds to pay all creditors in full and provide for a substantial distribution to common shareholders – which is unlikely. Some of these contracts contain anti-assignment clauses, some expressly allow assignment, others are silent. This being the case, they will likely resist any purported assignment of their contracts to the Buyer, and may seek to renegotiate those contracts when they learn of the sale, all to the detriment to the Buyer. The Buyer may not have realized this likely course of events at this time.

Your main objective in this transaction is to maximize the price that will be received by the Company for the sale of assets. You have advised Paul and Mary that, as directors and officers, their duty is to maximize the return to shareholders (or, if the company is insolvent or in the so-called "zone of insolvency," to maximize the return to creditors). This means that you want as many assets as possible to be included in the sale, and for the highest price to be obtained. For any present value analysis purposes – if payment is to be made over time -- the Company generally uses a 10% discount rate. You will want to emphasize the going concern value of the Company rather than the liquidation value of the assets.

Although there are really not enough data points to provide you with a standard, business valuation experts generally use a revenue (as there are no earnings) multiplier of between 2 to 4 for this sort of business.

The officers have instructed you to negotiate the best deal possible, and handle all the legal issues, turning to them for the business issues as they arise. They have indicated that they would like, at a minimum, for the sales price to be at least 1.5 times the book value of the assets, or approximately $25.5 million, which would leave room for some distributions to equity.

---

[23]   Note that you represent either the company or its owners and officers. You need to pay attention to conflict of interest issues, as well as the fiduciary duties of Paul and Mary to various constituencies.

Paul and Mary, individually, are primarily concerned with continued employment. They have been drawing salaries of $400,000 annually, and would like that to continue – although they understand that may not be possible. Paul is devoted to this business, and would like to stay on forever, as long as the acquirer will also hire Ron Olson, his "go-to guy". Ron currently makes $80,000 per year. Mary would like to stay on for up to a year and then transition on to other business opportunities and get away from so much contact with her former husband. Paul and Mary's instincts are to choose higher salaries for themselves over an increased purchase price payable to the company, but they have some sense of fiduciary duty and a desperate fear of lawsuits. They prefer cash payment over stock, but Paul in particular is willing to take up to 75% of his compensation in stock if the company will provide him with a position in its future.

Confidential Facts for Counsel for TakeAdvantageOfStudents, Inc.

TakeAdvantageOf Students' believes that acquiring HighSchoolToCollege's business and operating it as a division linked to its other sites will produce synergies that will translate into operating results far beyond those of any other company in the industry. As such, it is very important that the acquisition be of the business as a going concern and that relationships with vendors and strategic partners be maintained.

With that said, TakeAdvantageOfStudents does not want to pay more than it has to. It considers the book value of HighSchoolToCollege's assets to be high in comparison to their actual replacement or liquidation value. It has its doubts about the accuracy of the balance sheet valuations of intangibles, such as intellectual property and goodwill. It would like to purchase the company for a value of no more than $20 million, with as much of that value being paid in its own stock instead of cash, including the salaries of any insiders that are hired. It has more than enough treasury stock to fund the entire purchase, but realizes that this is unlikely. Currently, it would like to hire Paul and Mary and Ron Olson, their contract supervisor; but it wants to be in a position to terminate Paul and Mary (but not Ron), within no more than 6 months, and preferably 3 months, after the closing and a smooth transition. Although company executives believe that Mary is a repository of institutional knowledge and wish to be able to tap that asset in the future, they believe that Paul is an egotistical blowhard who has built the business on his enthusiastic marketing skills and is largely unnecessary to the

TakeAdvantageOfStudents business model. They would be happy to be rid of him as soon as the sale closes and the transaction is complete. TakeAdvantageOfStudents is a "lean and mean" organization, with its executives earning a flat $120,000 a year at all levels, with an adjustable bonus of stock awarded at the end of each calendar year. Those bonuses have ranged from $25,000 to $300,000 in value (of the stock, on the day it was awarded).

You have been told that, although there are really not enough data points to provide you with a standard, business valuation experts generally use a revenue multiplier of between 2 to 4 for this sort of business.

The officers have instructed you to negotiate the best deal possible, and handle all the legal issues, turning to them for the business issues as they arise.

Group Four completed this assignment with relative ease because of the manner that we approached the project. First, as buyer, I was in a position to play hard ball (because of the dynamics of an in-class assignment, the seller cannot just "walk away"). However, I trusted the sellers; mainly I trusted the sellers because I have a relationship with Ms. K that goes back a couple of years. Furthermore, Mr. E is very easy going and trustworthy. Therefore, our style was simple: get the job done. Our clients' interests were always our number one concern. But, "getting the job done" could was not far behind.

The document was completed early and through a group effort. Ms. K drafted the agreement on her computer. This draft came from re-typing the available example into her word processor, which was an arduous task but did force her to examine every position. Then, the group would get together and hammer out the provisions. This, of course, came after we had negotiated a purchase price. We had probably five, or so, meetings in which we hammered out the deal. We determined the time and place via email. Everyone was very accommodating to each other's needs. Once we met, it really was a group effort. Ms. K and I brought a critical eye towards that grammar and word use. Mr. E caught typos and was critical on the overall content of the document. Furthermore, our backgrounds tended to help in various areas (e.g., my background in Commercial Law helped draft the promissory note). Once again, if one of us felt a provision was vague and wanted insight, we trusted each other to ask what the provision meant. Once again, we realized that all our clients wanted the deal to get done.

The purchase price was $25,760,047. The break down goes as follows:

> Seller financing: $6,975,00 (with a $700,000 deposit)
> Assumption of liabilities: $11,983.759
> Accrued wages and taxes: $361,288
> Stock: 1,6100,000 shares at $4 a share

I (the buyer) assumed all liabilities for a dollar for dollar exchange. The rest broke down into negotiation and number crunching. The two issues that stood out in the negotiations were goodwill and the future revenue estimates. At the very least (determining that goodwill was non-existent and using the lowest revenue multiplier), the company should have sold for $20 million.[24] However, Mr. Edmunson was a tough negotiator, and brought the number up. In the end, as the buyer, I felt that my clients received a good deal.

---

24 I personally cannot see how a buyer could demand less than $20 million. Any reasonable seller would just walk away.